Your Office

Getting Started with Advanced Cases for Microsoft® Office 2010

Amy Kinser

BARRY WALKER

SANDRA McCORMACK

JENNIFER P. NIGHTINGALE

PEARSON

Boston   Columbus   Indianapolis   New York   San Francisco   Upper Saddle River
Amsterdam   Cape Town   Dubai   London   Madrid   Milan   Munich   Paris   Montreal   Toronto
Delhi   Mexico City   Sao Paulo   Sydney   Hong Kong   Seoul   Singapore   Taipei   Tokyo

Editor in Chief: Michael Payne
Acquisitions Editor: Samantha McAfee
Product Development Manager: Laura Burgess
Editorial Project Manager: Anne Garcia
Development Editor: Nancy Lamm
Editorial Assistant: Laura Karahalis
Digital Media Editor: Eric Hakanson
Director, Media Development: Cathi Profitko
Production Media Project Manager: John Cassar
VP/Director of Business & Technology Marketing: Patrice Jones
Marketing Manager: Nate Anderson
Marketing Coordinator: Susan Osterlitz
Marketing Assistant: Darshika Vyas

Managing Editor: Camille Trentacoste
Senior Production Project Manager: Rhonda Aversa
IT Procurement Lead: Natacha Moore
Senior Operations Manager/Site Lead: Nick Sklitsis
Senior Art Director: Jonathan Boylan
Manager of Rights & Permissions: Jenn Kennett
Senior Art Director: Jonathan Boylan
Cover Design: Anthony Gemmellaro
Interior Design: Anthony Gemmellaro
Composition: GEX Publishing Services
Full-Service Project Management: GEX Publishing Services

Credits and acknowledgments borrowed from other sources and reproduced, with permission, in this textbook appear on appropriate page within text.

Pearson Education Ltd., London
Pearson Education Singapore, Pte. Ltd
Pearson Education, Canada, Inc.
Pearson Education–Japan
Pearson Education Australia PTY, Limited

Pearson Education North Asia Ltd., Hong Kong
Pearson Educación de Mexico, S.A. de C.V.
Pearson Education Malaysia, Pte. Ltd.
Pearson Education, Upper Saddle River, New Jersey

Library of Congress Cataloging-in-Publication Data available upon request

10 9 8 7 6 5 4 3 2 1
ISBN-13: 978-0-13-267549-9
ISBN-10: 0-13-267549-8

About the Authors

Barry V. Walker

Barry holds B.A. degrees in Economics and Computer Science from the New York State University College at Oswego and a M.S. in Systems Management from the University of Southern California. After serving 7 years as an artillery officer, personnel officer, and quality control officer of recruiting in the United States Marine Corps, he has spent the past 29 years teaching technology at Monroe Community College and developing custom software solutions for businesses. He also loves spending time with his children and especially his grandsons, Wyatt, Harlan, Tobias, and Emmett.

I dedicate this series to my wife, Mary Catherine, for her unwavering faith, love, and support without which this text would not have been possible.

Barry Walker

Sandra M. McCormack

Sandra holds a B.S. degree in Biology from Rochester Institute of Technology and a M.S. in Management from Nazareth College. After many years as an adjunct instructor and independent consultant providing Scanning Electron Microscopy services for a wide variety of research projects, Sandra's career path took a turn that led her into full-time teaching. For the past 12 years she has been teaching Computer Information Systems courses at Monroe Community College. She is an Associate Professor in the Business Administration and Economics Department and serves as the CIS Discipline Coordinator. When not at school, Sandra can be found on the family's horse farm. She enjoys spending time with her husband Sean, adult children Collin, Katie, and Mary, and her adorable granddaughter, Marne.

I dedicate this project to my family and thank them for their love, support, and encouragement.

Sandra McCormack

Dr. Jennifer Paige Nightingale

Jennifer Nightingale, assistant professor at Duquesne University, has taught Information Systems Management since 2000. Before joining Duquesne University, she spent 15 years in industry with a focus in management and training. Her research expertise is in instructional technology, using technology as a teaching tool, and the impact of instructional technologies on student learning. She has earned numerous teaching and research honors and awards, holds an Ed.D. (instructional technology) and two M.S. degrees (information systems management and education) from Duquesne University, and a B.A. from the University of Pittsburgh.

To my parents, who always believed in and encouraged me. To my husband and best friend, who gave me support, patience, and love. To my brother and my hero—may you be watching from Heaven with joy in your heart.

Jennifer Nightingale

Amy S. Kinser, Esq., Series Editor

Amy holds a B.A. degree in Chemistry with a Business minor from Indiana University, and a J.D. from the Maurer School of Law, also at Indiana University. After working as an environmental chemist, starting her own technology consulting company, and practicing intellectual property law, she has spent the past 12 years teaching technology at the Kelley School of Business in Bloomington, Indiana. Currently, she serves as the Director of Computer Skills and Senior Lecturer at the Kelley School of Business at Indiana University. She also loves spending time with her two sons, Aidan and J. Matthew, and her husband J. Eric.

I dedicate this series to my Kinser Boyz for their unwavering love, support, and patience; to my parents and sister for their love; to my students for inspiring me; to Sam for believing in me; and to the instructors I hope this series will inspire!

Amy Kinser

Contents

ADVANCED CASES

WORKSHOP 1: Analyzing Business Problems   1

PREPARE CASE: Golf Nook Clothing Store: Sales, Inventory, and Customer Analysis   1

Define the Business Problem   2

  Planning Steps to Solve the Business Problem   2
    Problem Definition   2
  Creating the Queries   7
    Information Requirements   8
    Intrinsic Functions   9
    Determining the Starting Inventory   11
  Exporting Data to Excel for Analysis and Charting   16
    Analysis and Charting   17
  Create a Report of the Problem Solution   19
  Develop a Presentation of the Recommended Action   20
  Plan an Inventory Analysis   21
    Problem Definition   21
    Analysis Report   26
    Analysis Presentation   27
  Plan a Customer Analysis   27
    Problem Definition   27
Concept Check   36
Key Terms   36
Visual Summary   36
Practice   37
  Practice Case 1   37

WORKSHOP 2: Solving Business Problems   43

PREPARE CASE: My Sparkles: Developing a Business Plan, Creating a Financial Analysis, and Managing Customers and Inventory   43

Developing a Business Plan   44
  Building a Decision Support System   45
  Perform a Financial Analysis   45

Creating a Database   51
  Building the My Sparkles Database   51
  Working with Customer Data   56
  Requesting Additional Customer Data   59

Developing a Target Market   62
  Identifying the Target Market   63
    Updating the Database for Additional Customer Data   64

Creating a Persona   67

Analyzing the Company and Industry   69
  Developing a SWOT Analysis   69
  Analyzing an Industry Using Porter's Five Forces Model   72

Creating a Customer Loyalty Program   76

Compiling Your Business Plan   77
  Develop the Components of a Business Plan   78
Concept Check   84
Key Terms   84
Visual Summary   84
Practice   85
  Practice Case 1   85
  Practice Case 2   88

ADVANCED CASES MODULE 1 CAPSTONE   91

Perform   91
  Perform 1: Perform in Your Career   91
  Perform 2: Perform in Your Career   93
  Perform 3: How Others Perform   94
  Perform 4: Perform in Your Career   98

Glossary   103

Index   105

Acknowledgments

The *Your Office* team would like to thank the following reviewers who have invested time and energy to help shape this series from the very beginning, providing us with invaluable feedback through their comments, suggestions, and constructive criticism.

We'd like to thank our Editorial Board:

Marni Ferner
University of North Carolina, Wilmington

Jan Hime
University of Nebraska, Lincoln

Linda Kavanaugh
Robert Morris University

Mike Kelly
Community College of Rhode Island

Suhong Li
Bryant University

Sebena Masline
Florida State College of Jacksonville

Candace Ryder
Colorado State University

Cindi Smatt
Texas A&M University

Jill Weiss
Florida International University

We'd like to thank our class testers:

Melody Alexander
Ball State University

Karen Allen
Community College of Rhode Island

Charmayne Cullom
University of Northern Colorado

Christy Culver
Marion Technical College

Marni Ferner
University of North Carolina, Wilmington

Linda Fried
University of Colorado, Denver

Darren Hayes
Pace University

Jan Hime
University of Nebraska, Lincoln

Emily Holliday
Campbell University

Carla Jones
Middle Tennessee State Unversity

Mike Kelly
Community College of Rhode Island

David Largent
Ball State University

Freda Leonard
Delgado Community College

Suhong Li
Bryant Unversity

Sebena Masline
Florida State College of Jacksonville

Sandra McCormack
Monroe Community College

Sue McCrory
Missouri State Unversity

Patsy Parker
Southwest Oklahoma State Unversity

Alicia Pearlman
Baker College, Allen Park

Vickie Pickett
Midland College

Rose Pollard
Southeast Community College

Leonard Presby
William Paterson University

Amy Rutledge
Oakland University

Cindi Smatt
Texas A&M Unversity

Jill Weiss
Florida International Unversity

We'd like to thank our reviewers and focus group attendees:

Sven Aelterman
Troy University

Angel Alexander
Piedmont Technical College

Melody Alexander
Ball State University

Karen Allen
Community College of Rhode Island

Maureen Allen
Elon University

Wilma Andrews
Virginia Commonwealth University

Mazhar Anik
Owens Community College

David Antol
Harford Community College

Kirk Atkinson
Western Kentucky University

Barbara Baker
Indiana Wesleyan University

Kristi Berg
Minot State University

Kavuri Bharath
Old Dominion University

Ann Blackman
Parkland College

Jeanann Boyce
Montgomery College

Cheryl Brown
Delgado Community College West Bank Campus

Bonnie Buchanan
Central Ohio Technical College

Peggy Burrus
Red Rocks Community College

Richard Cacace
Pensacola State College

Margo Chaney
Carroll Community College

Shanan Chappell
College of the Albemarle, North Carolina

Kuan-Chou Chen
Purdue University, Calumet

David Childress
Ashland Community and Technical College

Keh-Wen Chuang
Purdue University North Central

Amy Clubb
Portland Community College

Bruce Collins
Davenport University

Charmayne Cullom
University of Northern Colorado

Juliana Cypert
Tarrant County College

Harold Davis
Southeastern Louisiana University

Jeff Davis
Jamestown Community College

Jennifer Day
Sinclair Community College

Anna Degtyareva
Mt. San Antonio College

Beth Deinert
Southeast Community College

Kathleen DeNisco
Erie Community College

Donald Dershem
Mountain View College

Bambi Edwards
Craven Community College

Elaine Emanuel
Mt. San Antonio College

Diane Endres
Ancilla College

Nancy Evans
Indiana University, Purdue University,
Indianapolis

Linda Fried
University of Colorado, Denver

Diana Friedman
Riverside Community College

Susan Fry
Boise State University

Virginia Fullwood
Texas A&M University, Commerce

Janos Fustos
Metropolitan State College of Denver

Saiid Ganjalizadeh
The Catholic University of America

Randolph Garvin
Tyler Junior College

Diane Glowacki
Tarrant County College

Jerome Gonnella
Northern Kentucky University

Connie Grimes
Morehead State University

Babita Gupta
California State University, Monterey Bay

Lewis Hall
Riverside City College

Jane Hammer
Valley City State University

Marie Hartlein
Montgomery County Community College

Darren Hayes
Pace Unversity

Paul Hayes
Eastern New Mexico Universtiy

Mary Hedberg
Johnson County Community College

Lynda Henrie
LDS Business College

Deedee Herrera
Dodge City Community College

Cheryl Hinds
Norfolk State University

Mary Kay Hinkson
Fox Valley Technical College

Margaret Hohly
Cerritos College

Brian Holbert
Spring Hill College

Susan Holland
Southeast Community College

Anita Hollander
University of Tennessee, Knoxville

Emily Holliday
Campbell University

Stacy Hollins
St. Louis Community College, Florissant Valley

Mike Horn
State University of New York, Geneseo

Christie Hovey
Lincoln Land Community College

Margaret Hvatum
St. Louis Community College Meramec

Jean Insinga
Middlesex Community College

Jon (Sean) Jasperson
Texas A&M University

Glen Jenewein
Kaplan University

Gina Jerry
Santa Monica College

Dana Johnson
North Dakota State University

Mary Johnson
Mt. San Antonio College

Linda Johnsonius
Murray State University

Carla Jones
Middle Tennessee State University

Susan Jones
Utah State University

Nenad Jukic
Loyola University, Chicago

Sali Kaceli
Philadelphia Biblical University

Sue Kanda
Baker College of Auburn Hills

Robert Kansa
Macomb Community College

Susumu Kasai
Salt Lake Community College

Debby Keen
University of Kentucky

Melody Kiang
California State Universtiy, Long Beach

Lori Kielty
College of Central Florida

Richard Kirk
Pensacola State College

Dawn Konicek
Blackhawk Tech

John Kucharczuk
Centennial College

David Largent
Ball State University

Frank Lee
Fairmont State University

Luis Leon
The University of Tennessee at Chattanooga

Freda Leonard
Delgado Community College

Julie Lewis
Baker College, Allen Park

Renee Lightner
Florida State College

John Lombardi
South University

Rhonda Lucas
Spring Hill College

Adriana Lumpkin
Midland College

Lynne Lyon
Durham College

Nicole Lytle
California State University, San Bernardino

Donna Madsen
Kirkwood Community College

Paul Martin
Harrisburg Area Community College

Cheryl Martucci
Diablo Valley College

Sherry Massoni
Harford Community College

Lee McClain
Western Washington University

Sandra McCormack
Monroe Community College

Sue McCrory
Missouri State University

Barbara Miller
University of Notre Dame

Michael O. Moorman
Saint Leo University

Alysse Morton
Westminster College

Elobaid Muna
University of Maryland Eastern Shore

Jackie Myers
Sinclair Community College

Bernie Negrete
Cerritos College

Melissa Nemeth
Indiana University, Purdue University, Indianapolis

Jennifer Nightingale
Duquesne University

Kathie O'Brien
North Idaho College

Patsy Parker
Southwestern Oklahoma State University

Laurie Patterson
University of North Carolina, Wilmington

Alicia Pearlman
Baker College

Diane Perreault
Sierra College and California State University, Sacramento

Vickie Pickett
Midland College

Marcia Polanis
Forsyth Technical Community College

Rose Pollard
Southeast Community College

Stephen Pomeroy
Norwich University

Leonard Presby
William Paterson University

Donna Reavis
Delta Career Education

Eris Reddoch
Pensacola State College

James Reddoch
Pensacola State College

Michael Redmond
La Salle University

Terri Rentfro
John A. Logan College

Vicki Robertson
Southwest Tennessee Community College

Dianne Ross
University of Louisiana at Lafayette

Ann Rowlette
Liberty University

Amy Rutledge
Oakland University

Joann Segovia
Winona State University

Eileen Shifflett
James Madison University

Sandeep Shiva
Old Dominion University

Robert Sindt
Johnson County Community College

Edward Souza
Hawaii Pacific University

Nora Spencer
Fullerton College

Alicia Stonesifer
La Salle University

Cheryl Sypniewski
Macomb Community College

Arta Szathmary
Bucks County Community College

Nasser Tadayon
Southern Utah Unversity

Asela Thomason
California State University Long Beach

Joyce Thompson
Lehigh Carbon Community College

Terri Tiedeman
Southeast Community College, Nebraska

Lewis Todd
Belhaven University

Barb Tollinger
Sinclair Community College

Allen Truell
Ball State University

Erhan Uskup
Houston Community College

Michelle Vlaich-Lee
Greenville Technical College

Barry Walker
Monroe Community College

Rosalyn Warren
Enterprise State Community College

Eric Weinstein
Suffolk County Community College

Lorna Wells
Salt Lake Community College

Rosalie Westerberg
Clover Park Technical College

Clemetee Whaley
Southwest Tennessee Community College

MaryLou Wilson
Piedmont Technical College

John Windsor
University of North Texas

Kathy Winters
University of Tennessee, Chattanooga

Nancy Woolridge
Fullerton College

Jensen Zhao
Ball State University

Martha Zimmer
University of Evansville

Molly Zimmer
University of Evansville

Matthew Zullo
Wake Technical Community College

Additionally, we'd like to thank our my**it**lab team for their tireless work:

Jerri Williams
my**it**lab content author

Ralph Moore
my**it**lab content author

LeeAnn Bates
my**it**lab content author

Jennifer Hurley
my**it**lab content author

Jessica Brandi
Associate Media Project Manager

Jaimie Howard
Media Producer

Cathi Profitko
Director, Media Development

Preface

The *Your Office* series is built upon the discovery that both instructors and students need a modern approach to teaching and learning Microsoft Office applications, an approach that weaves in a business context and focuses on using Office as a decision-making tool.

The process of developing this unique series for you, the modern student or instructor, required innovative ideas regarding the pedagogy and organization of the text. You learn best when doing—so you will be active from Page 1. Your learning goes to the next level when you are challenged to do more with less—your hand will be held at first, but progressively the cases require more from you. Since you care about how things work in the real world—in your classes, your future jobs, your personal life—these innovative features will help you progress from a basic understanding of Office to mastering each application, empowering you to perform with confidence when using Web 2.0 tools.

No matter what career you may choose to pursue in life, this series will give you the foundation to succeed. *Your Office* uses cases that will enable you to be immersed in a realistic business as you learn Office in the context of a running business scenario—the Painted Paradise Resort and Spa. You will immediately delve into the many interesting, smaller businesses in this resort (golf course, spa, restaurants, hotel, etc.) to learn how a business or organization uses Office. You will learn how to make Office work for you now as a student and in your future career.

Today, the experience of working with Office is not isolated to working in a job in a cubicle. Your physical office is wherever you are with a laptop or a mobile device. Office has changed. It's modern. It's mobile. It's personal. And when you learn these valuable skills and master Office, you are able to make Office your own. The title of this series is a promise to you, the student: Our goal is to make Microsoft Office *Your Office*.

Key Features

- **Starting and Ending Files:** Before every case, the Starting and Ending Files are identified for students. Starting Files identify exactly which Student Data Files are needed to complete each case. Ending Files are provided to show students the naming conventions they should use when saving their files.

- **Workshop Objectives List:** The learning objectives to be achieved as students work through the workshop. Page numbers are included for easy reference.

- **Active Text:** Appears throughout the workshop and is easily distinguishable from explanatory text by the shaded background. Active Text helps students quickly identify what steps they need to follow to complete the workshop Prepare Case.

- **Real World Advice Box:** A boxed feature that appears throughout the workshop where applicable, offering advice and best practices for general use of important Office skills. The goal is to instruct students as a manager might in a future job.

- **Consider This**: In-text questions or topics for discussion set apart from the main explanatory text, that allow students to step back from the project and think about the skills and the applications of what they are learning and how they might be used in the future.

- **Concept Check:** A section at the end of each workshop made up of approximately five concept-related questions that are short answer or open ended for students to review.

- **Visual Summary:** A visual representation of the important skills learned in the workshop. Call-outs and brief explanations illustrate important buttons or skills demonstrated in a screenshot of the final solution for the Workshop Prepare Case. Intended as a visual review of the objectives learned in the workshop; it is mapped to the objectives using page numbers so students can easily find the section of text to refer to for a refresher.

Instructor Resources

The Instructor's Resource Center, available at www.pearsonhighered.com includes the following:

- Annotated Solution Files with Scorecards assist with grading the Prepare, Practice, Problem Solve, and Perform Cases.

- Data and Solution Files

- Rubrics for Perform Cases in Microsoft Word format enable instructors to easily grade open-ended assignments with no definite solution.

- PowerPoint Presentations with notes for each workshop are included for out-of-class study or review.

- Complete Test Bank, also available in TestGen format

- Workshop-level Problem Solve Cases for more assessment on the objectives on an individual workshop level

- Scripted Lectures that provide instructors with a lecture outline that mirrors the Workshop Prepare Case

Student Resources

Pearson's Companion Website

www.pearsonhighered.com/youroffice offers expanded IT resources and downloadable supplements. Students can find the following self-study tools for each workshop:

- Online Study Guide
- Workshop Objectives
- Glossary
- Workshop Objectives Review
- Web Resources
- Student Data Files
- Additional Cases with data files and instructions

my**it**lab for Office 2010 is a solution designed by professors for professors that allows easy delivery of Office courses with defensible assessment and outcomes-based training. The new **Your Office 2010** system will seamlessly integrate online assessment, training, and projects with my**it**lab for Microsoft Office 2010!

my**it**lab for Office 2010 Features...

- **Assessment and training built to match *Your Office 2010*** instructional content so that my**it**lab works with Your Office to help students make Office their own.

- **Both project-based and skill-based assessment and training** allow instructors to test and train students on complete exercises or individual Office application skills.

- **Full course management functionality** which includes all instructor and student resources, a complete Gradebook, and the ability to run a variety of reports including detailed student clickstream data.

- **The most open, realistic, high-fidelity simulation** of Office 2010 makes students feel like they are learning Office, not just a simulation.

- **Grader, a live-in-the-application project-grading tool,** enables instructors to assign projects taken from the end-of-chapter material and additional projects included in the instructor resources. These are graded automatically, with detailed feedback provided to both instructors and students.

Visual Walk-Through

Clear Objectives with page numbers identify the learning objectives to be achieved as students work through the workshop. Students see these first at the workshop opener, and again at the Visual Summary.

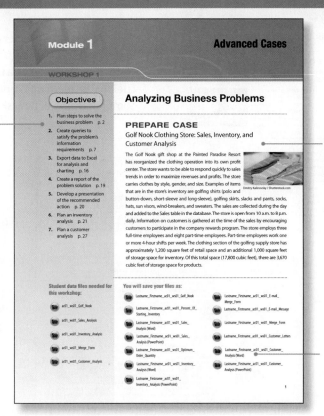

The **Running Business Scenario** is the basis of the Prepare Case. This illustrates for students how businesses use Microsoft Office in the real world.

Starting and Ending Data Files clearly list the names of starting data files and naming conventions for the ending solution files prior to each case.

Concept Check is at the end of each workshop and is made up of approximately five concept-related questions that are short answer or open-ended.

The **Visual Summary** is a quick visual review of the objectives learned in the workshop, and is mapped to the Workshop using page numbers so students can easily refer back to for a refresher.

Throughout the Workshop there are three different cases characterized by the level of instruction or hand-holding that students receive. The goal of the progression of these cases is to take students from an introductory level all the way to mastery, so students can learn to make Office their own.

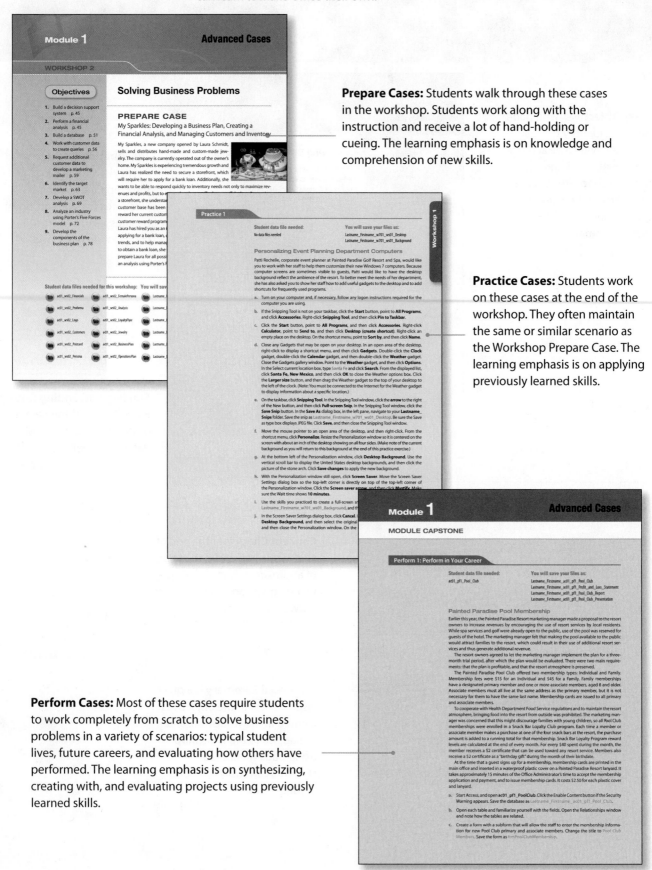

Prepare Cases: Students walk through these cases in the workshop. Students work along with the instruction and receive a lot of hand-holding or cueing. The learning emphasis is on knowledge and comprehension of new skills.

Practice Cases: Students work on these cases at the end of the workshop. They often maintain the same or similar scenario as the Workshop Prepare Case. The learning emphasis is on applying previously learned skills.

Perform Cases: Most of these cases require students to work completely from scratch to solve business problems in a variety of scenarios: typical student lives, future careers, and evaluating how others have performed. The learning emphasis is on synthesizing, creating with, and evaluating projects using previously learned skills.

Quick Reference Boxes appear throughout the Workshop, summarizing generic or alternative instructions on how to accomplish a task. This feature enables students to quickly find important skills.

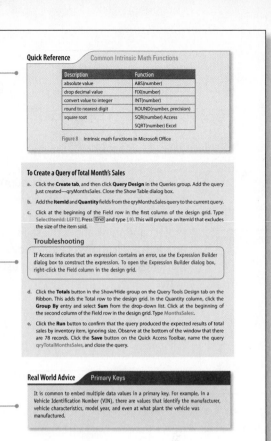

Quick Reference — Common Intrinsic Math Functions

Description	Function
absolute value	ABS(number)
drop decimal value	FIX(number)
convert value to integer	INT(number)
round to nearest digit	ROUND(number, precision)
square root	SQR(number) Access
	SQRT(number) Excel

Figure 8   Intrinsic math functions in Microsoft Office

To Create a Query of Total Month's Sales

a. Click the **Create tab**, and then click **Query Design** in the Queries group. Add the query just created—qryMonthsSales. Close the Show Table dialog box.

b. Add the **ItemId** and **Quantity** fields from the qryMonthsSales query to the current query.

c. Click at the beginning of the Field row in the first column of the design grid. Type SelectItemId: LEFT([. Press [End] and type],9). This will produce an ItemId that excludes the size of the item sold.

Troubleshooting

If Access indicates that an expression contains an error, use the Expression Builder dialog box to construct the expression. To open the Expression Builder dialog box, right-click the Field column in the design grid.

d. Click the **Totals** button in the Show/Hide group on the Query Tools Design tab on the Ribbon. This adds the Total row to the design grid. In the Quantity column, click the **Group By** entry and select **Sum** from the drop-down list. Click at the beginning of the second column of the Field row in the design grid. Type MonthsSales:.

e. Click the **Run** button to confirm that the query produced the expected results of total sales by inventory item, ignoring size. Observe at the bottom of the window that there are 78 records. Click the **Save** button on the Quick Access Toolbar, name the query qryTotalMonthsSales, and close the query.

Real World Advice — Primary Keys

It is common to embed multiple data values in a primary key. For example, in a Vehicle Identification Number (VIN), there are values that identify the manufacturer, vehicle characteristics, model year, and even at what plant the vehicle was manufactured.

10   Module 1   Advanced Cases

Troubleshooting is a note in the Active Text that helps students work around common pitfalls or errors that might occur.

Real World Advice Boxes appear throughout the workshop, offering advice and best practices for general use of important Office skills. The goal is to instruct students as a manager might in a future career.

To Create the My Sparkles Database

a. Click the **Start** button, and then select **Access 2010**. Click **Blank database**. Browse to where you are storing your data files, and name your database Lastname_Firstname_ ac01_ws02_MySparkles, replacing Lastname_Firstname with your own name. Click the **Create** button to create the database.

b. Design a table to store product categories. Create appropriate fields that will describe the inventory categories and the gender for which they relate, and then assign a field to be the primary key. For all fields, enter appropriate data type descriptions, field sizes, and other field properties as needed. Save your table as tblCategory. Enter the following inventory categories into the table, and then add two new categories along with the appropriate gender. Be sure to resize fields as needed so all data are visible. Close tblCategory.

Category Name	Gender
Earrings	Women
Bracelet	Both
Necklace	Both
Ring	Both

c. Design a table to store products. Choose appropriate fields that would describe the inventory categories, and then assign a field to be the primary key. For all fields, enter appropriate data type descriptions, field sizes, captions, and other field properties as needed. Save your table as tblProduct. Enter the products into the table by importing the data from the Product Pricing worksheet, and then add two new products for one of the new categories that you added. Be sure to resize fields as needed so all data are visible. Close tblProduct.

d. Design a table to store yearly forecasted quantities. Choose appropriate fields that would describe the forecasted inventory quantities, and then assign a field to be the primary key. For all fields, enter appropriate data type descriptions, field sizes, and other field properties as needed. Include one data validation rule. Save your table as tblForecast. Design the table so Laura can use it from year to year without deleting any existing data. Enter the data into the table by importing the data from the Product Pricing worksheet, and then be sure to resize fields as needed so all data are visible. Close tblForecast.

e. Create relationships between the tables as appropriate and enforce referential integrity.

SIDE NOTE
Entering Numbers into Validation Rules
When entering numbers or currency into a validation rule, do not enter symbols such as commas or a dollar sign.

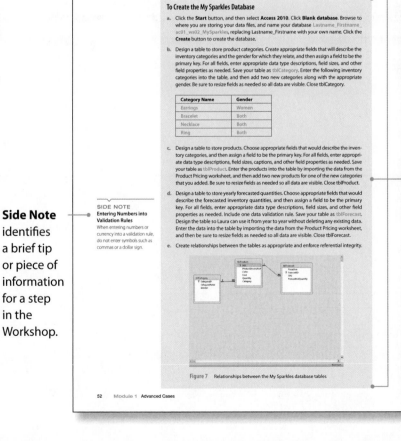

Figure 7   Relationships between the My Sparkles database tables

52   Module 1   Advanced Cases

Side Note identifies a brief tip or piece of information for a step in the Workshop.

Active Text Boxes appear throughout the Workshop and are easily distinguishable from explanatory text by the shaded background. Active Text helps students quickly identify what steps they need to follow to complete the Prepare Case and gets them working from start to finish.

Consider This is an in-text question or topic for discussion that allows students to step back from the project and think about the skills and the applications of what they are learning and how that might be used in the future.

CONSIDER THIS | **The United States vs. Microsoft Corporation**

In 1999, U.S. District Judge Thomas Penfield Jackson declared Microsoft a monopoly and rejected the company's defense that its actions have not harmed consumers. Microsoft holds more than 90% of the market share for PC operating systems, and Judge Jackson stated that this has caused consumer harm by "distorting competition." Jackson explained that three main facts indicate that Microsoft relishes in monopoly power. First, Microsoft's share of the market for Intel-compatible PC operating systems is extremely large and steady. Second, Microsoft's prevailing market share is secure because of a high barrier to entry. Third, and essentially as a product of that barrier, Microsoft's customers lack a feasible alternative to Windows. Do you think Microsoft is a monopoly? It would cost millions if not billions of dollars to enter this market. Is Microsoft simply a product of its industry? Should it be blamed because competitors do not have the funding needed to enter the market?

Suppliers are the companies that supply materials and other products to organizations within the industry. The price of items purchased from suppliers—such as raw materials if the company manufactures goods or inventory if it sells finished products—can have a substantial impact on an organization's profitability. If suppliers have high bargaining power over an organization, then in theory the organization's industry is less attractive. When determining the bargaining power of suppliers, consider the following factors:

- There are many buyers and few suppliers.
- There are undifferentiated, highly valued products.
- Suppliers threaten to integrate forward into the industry, such as brand manufacturers threatening to open retail outlets.
- Buyers do not threaten to integrate backward into supply.
- The industry is not a crucial customer group to the suppliers.

Buyers are the people or organizations who create demand in the industry. The bargaining power of customers is their ability to put an organization under pressure, which also affects the customer's understanding of price changes. When determining the bargaining power of buyers, consider the following factors to determine whether the bargaining power of buyers is high:

- There are few buyers and many sellers.
- Switching costs are low.
- Buyers can easily create the seller's product themselves.
- Customers can purchase large volumes of identical products from the seller.
- Substitute products are available on the market.
- The customer is price conscious and well-educated about the product.

The threat of substitutes is the availability of a product that a consumer can purchase in place of another product that offers similar benefits. According to Porter, the threat of substitutes shapes the competitive structure of an industry. Alternatively, the shortage of similar substitute products makes an industry less competitive and increases the potential profit for the organizations in the industry. For example, consider the beverage industry because of the tremendous number of competitors. Pepsi would not be a substitute for Coca-Cola; however, coffee, tea, milk, juice, and water would be. The threat of substitute products depends on the following factors:

- Buyers' willingness to substitute
- The relative price and performance of substitutes
- The costs of switching to substitutes

Dear Students,

If you want an edge over the competition, make it personal. Whether you love sports, travel, the stock market, or ballet, your passion is personal to you. Capitalizing on your passion leads to success. You live in a global marketplace, and your competition is global. The honors students in China exceed the total number of students in North America. Skills can help set you apart, but passion will make you stand above. *Your Office* is the tool to harness your passion's true potential.

In prior generations, personalization in a professional setting was discouraged. You had a "work" life and a "home" life. As the Series Editor, I write to you about the vision for *Your Office* from my laptop, on my couch, in the middle of the night when inspiration struck me. My classroom and living room are my office. Life has changed from generations before us.

So, let's get personal. My degrees are not in technology, but chemistry and law. I helped put myself through school by working full time in various jobs, including a successful technology consulting business that continues today. My generation did not grow up with computers, but I did. My father was a network administrator for the military. So, I was learning to program in Basic before anyone had played Nintendo's Duck Hunt or Tetris. Technology has always been one of my passions from a young age. In fact, I now tell my husband: don't buy me jewelry for my birthday, buy me the latest gadget on the market!

In my first law position, I was known as the Office guru to the extent that no one gave me a law assignment for the first two months. Once I submitted the assignment, my supervisor remarked, "Wow, you don't just know how to leverage technology, but you really know the law too." I can tell you novel-sized stories from countless prior students in countless industries who gained an edge from using Office as a tool. Bringing technology to your passion makes you well rounded and a cut above the rest, no matter the industry or position.

I am most passionate about teaching, in particular teaching technology. I come from many generations of teachers, including my mother who is a kindergarten teacher. For over 12 years, I have found my dream job passing on my passion for teaching, technology, law, science, music, and life in general at the Kelley School of Business at Indiana University. I have tried to pass on the key to engaging passion to my students. I have helped them see what differentiates them from all the other bright students vying for the same jobs.

Microsoft Office is a tool. All of your competition will have learned Microsoft Office to some degree or another. Some will have learned it to an advanced level. Knowing Microsoft Office is important, but it is also fundamental. Without it, you will not be considered for a position.

Today, you step into your first of many future roles bringing Microsoft Office to your dream job working for Painted Paradise Resort and Spa. You will delve into the business side of the resort and learn how to use *Your Office* to maximum benefit.

Don't let the context of a business fool you. If you don't think of yourself as a business person, you have no need to worry. Whether you realize it or not, everything is business. If you want to be a nurse, you are entering the health care industry. If you want to be a football player in the NFL, you are entering the business of sports as entertainment. In fact, if you want to be a stay-at-home parent, you are entering the business of a family household where *Your Office* still gives you an advantage. For example, you will be able to prepare a budget in Excel and analyze what you need to do to afford a trip to Disney World!

At Painted Paradise Resort and Spa, you will learn how to make Office yours through four learning levels designed to maximize your understanding. You will Prepare, Practice, and Problem Solve your tasks. Then, you will astound when you Perform your new talents. You will be challenged through questions and gain insight through Real World Advice.

There is something more. You want success in what you are passionate about in your life. It is personal for you. In this position at Painted Paradise Resort and Spa, you will gain your personal competitive advantage that will stay with you for the rest of your life—*Your Office*.

Sincerely,

Amy Kinser

Series Editor

Welcome to the Painted Paradise Resort and Spa Team!

Welcome to your new office at Painted Paradise Resort and Spa, where we specialize in painting perfect getaways. As the Chief Technology Officer, I am excited to have staff dedicated to the Microsoft Office integration between all the areas of the resort. Our team is passionate about our paradise, and I hope you find this to be your dream position here!

Painted Paradise is a resort and spa in New Mexico catering to business people, romantics, families, and anyone who just needs to get away. Inside our resort are many distinct areas. Many of these areas operate as businesses in their own right but must integrate with the other areas of the resort. The main areas of the resort are as follows.

- The **Hotel** is overseen by our Chief Executive Officer, William Mattingly, and is at the core of our business. The hotel offers a variety of accommodations, ranging from individual rooms to a grand villa suite. Further, the hotel offers packages including spa, golf, and special events.

  Room rates vary according to size, season, demand, and discount. The hotel has discounts for typical groups, such as AARP. The hotel also has a loyalty program where guests can earn free nights based on frequency of visits. Guests may charge anything from the resort to the room.

- **Red Bluff Golf Course** is a private world-class golf course and pro shop. The golf course has services such as golf lessons from the famous golf pro John Schilling and playing packages. Also, the golf course attracts local residents. This requires variety in pricing schemes to accommodate both local and hotel guests. The pro shop sells many retail items online.

  The golf course can also be reserved for special events and tournaments. These special events can be in conjunction with a wedding, conference, meetings, or other event covered by the event planning and catering area of the resort.

- **Turquoise Oasis Spa** is a full-service spa. Spa services include haircuts, pedicures, massages, facials, body wraps, waxing, and various other spa services—typical to exotic. Further, the spa offers private consultation, weight training (in the fitness center), a water bar, meditation areas, and steam rooms. Spa services are offered both in the spa and in the resort guest's room.

  Turquoise Oasis Spa uses top-of-the-line products and some house-brand products. The retail side offers products ranging from candles to age-defying home treatments. These products can also be purchased online. Many of the hotel guests who fall in love with the house-brand soaps, lotions, candles, and other items appreciate being able to buy more at any time.

  The spa offers a multitude of packages including special hotel room packages that include spa treatments. Local residents also use the spa. So, the spa guests are not limited to hotel guests. Thus, the packages also include pricing attractive to the local community.

- **Painted Treasures Gift Shop** has an array of items available for purchase, from toiletries to clothes to presents for loved ones back home including a healthy section of kids' toys for traveling business people. The gift shop sells a small sampling from the spa, golf course pro shop, and local New Mexico culture. The gift shop also has a small section of snacks and drinks. The gift shop has numerous part-time employees including students from the local college.

- The **Event Planning & Catering** area is central to attracting customers to the resort. From weddings to conferences, the resort is a popular destination. The resort has a substantial number of staff dedicated to planning, coordinating, setting up, catering, and maintaining these events. The resort has several facilities that can accommodate large groups. Packages and prices vary by size, room, and other services such as catering. Further, the Event Planning & Catering team works closely with local vendors for floral decorations, photography, and other event or wedding typical needs. However, all catering must go through the resort (no outside catering permitted). Lastly, the resort stocks several choices of decorations, table arrangements, and centerpieces. These range from professional, simple, themed, and luxurious.

- **Indigo5** and the **Silver Moon Lounge**, a world-class restaurant and lounge that is overseen by the well-known Chef Robin Sanchez. The cuisine is balanced and modern. From steaks to pasta to local southwestern meals, Indigo5 attracts local patrons in addition to resort guests. While the catering function is separate from the restaurant—though menu items may be shared—the restaurant does support all room service for the resort. The resort also has smaller food venues onsite such as the Terra Cotta Brew coffee shop in the lobby.

Currently, these areas are using Office to various degrees. In some areas, paper and pencil are still used for most business functions. Others have been lucky enough to have some technology savvy team members start Microsoft Office Solutions.

Using your skills, I am confident that you can help us integrate and use Microsoft Office on a whole new level! I hope you are excited to call Painted Paradise Resort and Spa *Your Office*.

Looking forward to working with you more closely!

Aidan Matthews

Aidan Matthews
Chief Technology Officer

Objectives

1. Plan steps to solve the business problem   p. 2

2. Create queries to satisfy the problem's information requirements   p. 7

3. Export data to Excel for analysis and charting   p. 16

4. Create a report of the problem solution   p. 19

5. Develop a presentation of the recommended action   p. 20

6. Plan an inventory analysis   p. 21

7. Plan a customer analysis   p. 27

Analyzing Business Problems

PREPARE CASE

Golf Nook Clothing Store: Sales, Inventory, and Customer Analysis

The Golf Nook gift shop at the Painted Paradise Resort has reorganized the clothing operation into its own profit center. The store wants to be able to respond quickly to sales trends in order to maximize revenues and profits. The store carries clothes by style, gender, and size. Examples of items that are in the store's inventory are golfing shirts (polo and

Dmitry Kalinovsky / Shutterstock.com

button-down, short-sleeve and long-sleeve), golfing skirts, slacks and pants, socks, hats, sun visors, wind-breakers, and sweaters. The sales are collected during the day and added to the Sales table in the database. The store is open from 10 a.m. to 8 p.m. daily. Information on customers is gathered at the time of the sales by encouraging customers to participate in the company rewards program. The store employs three full-time employees and eight part-time employees. Part-time employees work one or more 4-hour shifts per week. The clothing section of the golfing supply store has approximately 1,200 square feet of retail space and an additional 1,000 square feet of storage space for inventory. Of this total space (17,800 cubic feet), there are 3,670 cubic feet of storage space for products.

Student data files needed for this workshop:

 ac01_ws01_Golf_Nook

 ac01_ws01_Sales_Analysis

 ac01_ws01_Inventory_Analysis

 ac01_ws01_Merge_Form

 ac01_ws01_Customer_Analysis

You will save your files as:

 Lastname_Firstname_ac01_ws01_Golf_Nook

 Lastname_Firstname_ac01_ws01_Percent_Of_Starting_Inventory

 Lastname_Firstname_ac01_ws01_Sales_Analysis (Word)

 Lastname_Firstname_ac01_ws01_Sales_Analysis (PowerPoint)

 Lastname_Firstname_ac01_ws01_Optimum_Order_Quantity

 Lastname_Firstname_ac01_ws01_Inventory_Analysis (Word)

 Lastname_Firstname_ac01_ws01_Inventory_Analysis (PowerPoint)

 Lastname_Firstname_ac01_ws01_E-mail_Merge_Form

 Lastname_Firstname_ac01_ws01_E-mail_Message

 Lastname_Firstname_ac01_ws01_Merge_Form

 Lastname_Firstname_ac01_ws01_Customer_Letters

 Lastname_Firstname_ac01_ws01_Customer_Analysis (Word)

 Lastname_Firstname_ac01_ws01_Customer_Analysis (PowerPoint)

Define the Business Problem

A business will regularly be confronted by challenges and obstacles to achieving its business goals. These challenges and obstacles are **business problems** that need to be resolved. The store manager, Susan Williams, has requested that an analysis be done to identify ways to increase sales of the most popular items that are being purchased on a monthly basis. An item is considered "popular" when over half of the in-store **inventory** is sold during one month and the item has not been previously placed on sale due to sales inactivity. A store's inventory consists of products stored and maintained for sale to customers. Using the available information in an Access database, along with the capabilities of an Excel workbook, you will complete the requested analysis. Upon completion of the analysis, you will create a written report using a Word document that will clearly describe the problem, relevant background information, data sources selected from the database and why they were selected, the analysis process, how the queries of the database were developed and how the data were imported to Excel, how the data were manipulated in Excel, and your conclusions and recommendations. You will then use the report information to create a PowerPoint presentation for the store manager.

Planning Steps to Solve the Business Problem

The first step in this process is to work through the planning steps for solving a problem. The **planning steps** are:

1. Defining the problem. This is a clean statement of what you are solving. Ideally it should include the measurable criteria that will be used to assess the proposed solution.
2. Identifying what you know and need to know to solve the problem. This will include data provided to you, data you need to acquire, formulas, and calculations that will be performed.
3. Developing the solution. This is the collection of step-by-step actions that will be carried out when solving the problem. This is the essential step in problem solving, and is the key skill that organizations look for in their employees.
4. Documenting and presenting your solution or recommendation. This communication of the problem-solving process provides the justification for how you recommend that the problem be resolved to the satisfaction of the criteria, or explains why the problem solution is unattainable.

Problem Definition

The Golf Nook needs to determine which products in inventory have been successful products. The criterion is that more than 50 percent of the product in inventory is sold over the course of the month. If the Golf Nook has 100 of an item in its inventory on the first of the month and 51 or more are sold during the month, the product is considered a "popular" product.

CONSIDER THIS | **Performance Criteria**

The criteria used to make a decision, such as whether a product is popular, could be any indicators of change. Examples might be a weekly increase in absolute sales over two weeks or more, or monthly sales that are above the monthly average by more than 10 percent. Whatever standard is selected, the next questions are: How are these changes going to be identified? What are some other possible indicators of change in sales, and how could they be identified?

The Golf Nook database contains the data values needed for analysis. The database is composed of several tables that contain data on the customers, employees, inventory, suppliers, and sales.

This database is normalized to help ensure the integrity of the data. **A normalized** database will include the natural relationships that exist among the entities—customers, sales, employees, inventory, and suppliers. This also minimizes the multiple appearances of data values—**data redundancy**—within the database. Redundancy can produce data anomalies. **Data anomalies** occur when the data value for an entity appears twice in different locations—tables—and those two data values are not the same. For example, the customer's home phone number appears in the customer table as (508) 555-7834 and in the sales table as (508) 555-6322. The customer table value is the one provided when the customer made his first purchase. The customer then gets a new phone number, and that number is recorded with the most recent sale. The database now has conflicting data. The solution is to ensure that the home phone number appears in only one table, in this case the customer table, as there might be multiple sales entries for a single customer.

The sales data are stored in two tables, tblSale and tblSaleItem. The information common to all sale items are in the tblSale table and the information unique to one sale item is stored in the tblSaleItem table. The data in the tables are linked by common fields called primary key fields and foreign key fields. This is called a **relationship**, and it is the foundation of a relational database such as those created in Access.

You should familiarize yourself with the database and its tables as shown in Figure 1. When unfamiliar with a database, examining the data and tables in the database is crucial. Understanding the database directly impacts the analysis and results. Thus, failure to understand the data often leads to erroneous analysis.

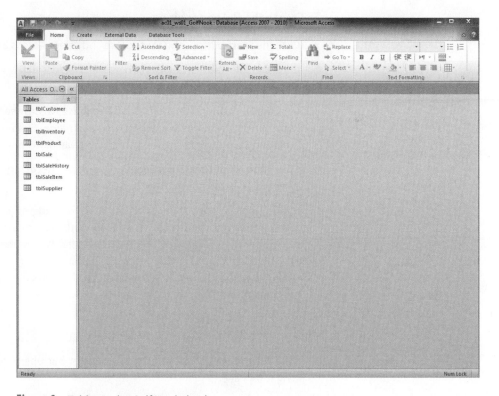

Figure 1   Tables in the Golf Nook database

The fields shown in Figure 2 were used to create the tblCustomer table structure in the Access database.

Field Name	Data Type
ID	AutoNumber(Long Integer)
LastName	Text
FirstName	Text
Address	Text
City	Text
State	Text
ZipCode	Text
ContactPhoneNumber	Text
CorporatePhoneNumber	Text
MobilePhoneNumber	Text
StartDate	Date/Time
E-mailAddress	Text

Figure 2   tblCustomer table record structure

In this section, you will create relationships.

To Create the Relationships

a. Click the **Start** button, and then locate and select **Access 2010**.

b. Click the **File tab**, click **Open**, locate and select **ac01_ws01_Golf_Nook**, and then click **Open**.

c. Click the **File tab**, and then click **Save Database As**. Browse to where you are storing your student files. In the File name box, type Lastname_Firstname_ac01_ws01_Golf_Nook, replacing Lastname_Firstname with your actual name and then click **Save**.

d. Click **Enable Content** in the Security Warning, if necessary.

e. Double-click the **tblCustomer** table to open it in Datasheet view. Review the fields and the data values. The first record is used to identify employee sales. The second record is used to identify a cash sale where the customer did not wish to identify herself. Switch to Design view and review the fields and their data types and properties as shown in Figure 2. Close the table. Do not save any changes. Repeat this for each of the remaining tables. It is important to close all tables because you cannot modify relationships of an open table.

Troubleshooting

If the tables are not visible, click the Shutter Bar Open/Close button to expand the Navigation Pane.

f. Click the **Database Tools tab** on the Ribbon and then click **Relationships** in the Relationships group. Add each of the tables to the Relationships window. Position and size the tables as shown in Figure 3.

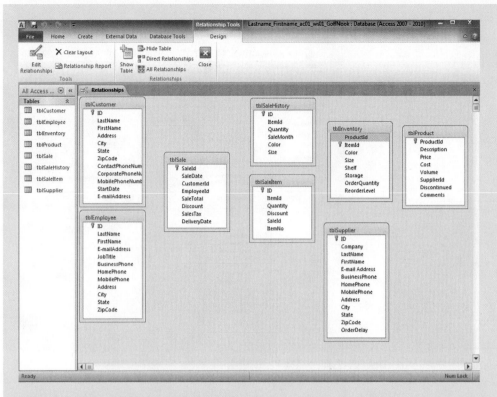

Figure 3 Tables in Relationships window

g. Click the **ID** field in the tblCustomer table. Drag onto the **CustomerID** field in the tblSale table and then release. This creates a relationship between the tblCustomer table and the tblSale table by dragging the ID field from the tblCustomer table and dropping it on the CustomerID field in the tblSale table. The Edit Relationships dialog box will open. Click the **Enforce Referential Integrity** check box. Click **Create**.

Troubleshooting

The error message in Figure 4 will appear because there is a conflict in the data types of the two fields. The data types of the two fields must match. You should open each of the tables in Design view to determine the field data types by checking the format in the Field Properties pane.

h. Change the Field Size of the CustomerID field in the tblSale table to Long Integer to match the format of the ID field in the tblCustomer table, and then save the table structure changes. A warning message will be displayed announcing that any decimal portion of a data value will be lost. None of the identifier values have a decimal value, so click **OK**. Close the tables and return to the Relationships window. Repeat the steps to create the relationship as stated in Step g.

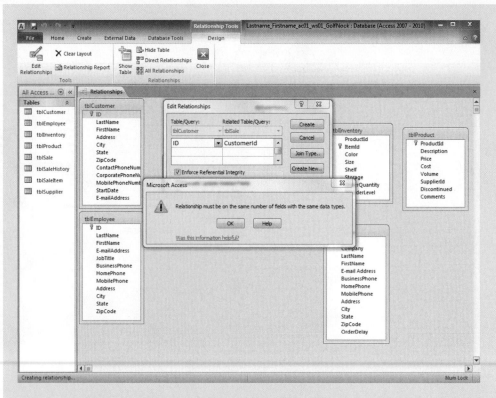

Figure 4   Data type mismatch between tblCustomer.ID and tblSale.CustomerId

i. Create a relationship between the **ID** field in the tblEmployee table and the **EmployeeID** field in the tblSale table. As noted in Step h, the EmployeeID field is a Number field with a format of Double. The EmployeeID values are all whole numbers, so the Double must be changed to a Long Integer, and the table structure changes saved and then complete the relationship above.

j. Create a relationship between the **SaleId** field in the tblSale table and the **SaleId** field in the tblSaleItem table. Be sure to enforce referential integrity.

k. Create a relationship between the **ItemId** field in the tblSaleItem table and the **ItemId** field in the tblInventory table. Be sure to enforce referential integrity.

l. Create a relationship between the **ItemId** field in the tblSaleHistory table and the **ItemId** field in the tblInventory table. Be sure to enforce referential integrity.

m. Create a relationship between the **ID** field in the tblSupplier table and the **SupplierId** field in the tblProduct table. Be sure to enforce referential integrity.

n. Create a relationship between the **ProductId** field in the tblInventory table and the **ProductId** field in the tblProduct table. Do not select Enforce Referential Integrity. The Relationships window should now look similar to Figure 5. These relationships will be applied automatically as tables are added to a query and a report. Close the Relationships window, saving changes.

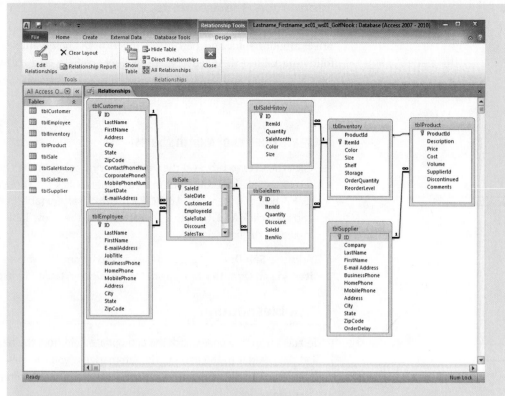

Figure 5 Tables and relationships in the Golf Nook database

CONSIDER THIS | **Record Identifiers**

The record identifiers in the tblCustomer, tblEmployee, and tblSupplier tables are system-generated primary keys. Because there are no naturally occurring values in these records that could serve as a primary key, a system-generated key is established. These entities might not even know the values of their primary key. What data have you encountered in your life that do not have a naturally occurring unique identifier?

Creating the Queries

For this problem, the goal is to determine those products in the inventory that have had a total sales amount greater than 50 percent of the starting inventory. It is assumed that no orders have been received during the previous month. How to relax this restriction will be discussed later. Additionally, sales to employees will be ignored, since the goal is to influence sales to customers.

The database needs to be queried in order to answer this question. This might require multiple queries. For example, the total sales for each product in inventory for the current month are needed.

Also, the month's starting inventory for each product in the inventory is needed. With these values, it is possible to determine which products satisfy the criteria of sales greater than 50 percent of the starting inventory.

The information that is needed is not available in only one table, but is available in two or more tables.

Information Requirements

First identify the data that are needed for the report: product ID, description, product price, amount sold, and percent of inventory. These values are going to come from the following tables: tblInventory, tblProduct, tblSale, and tblSaleItem. The common field will be the product ID. In this section, you will create queries.

To Create Queries of Month's Sales

a. Click the **Create tab**, and then click **Query Design** in the Queries group. Add the two tables **tblSale** and **tblSaleItem** to the query. Click the **tblSale** table in the Show Table dialog box, and then click **Add**. Click the **tblSaleItem** table in the Show Table dialog box, and then click **Add**. Click the **Close** button in the Show Table dialog box. The tables are joined on the fields SaleId.

b. Add the **SaleDate** and **CustomerId** fields from the tblSale table, and then add the **ItemId** and **Quantity** fields from the tblSaleItem table to the query.

Troubleshooting

To add a field to a query, click the appropriate field from the field list in the workspace, and then drag it to the design grid. Alternatively, you can double-click the field from the field list in the workspace, and the field will be added to the first empty column in the design grid.

c. In the Criteria row in the SaleDate column, type between 6/1/2013 and 6/30/2013.

d. In the Criteria row in the CustomerId column, type >1. This will exclude employee sales. The query design should be as shown in Figure 6.

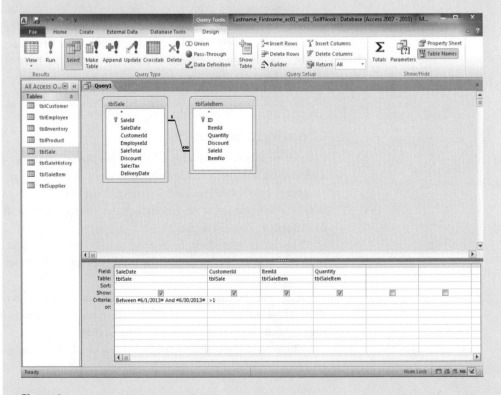

Figure 6   Month's Sales Query in Design view

e. Click the **Run** button in the Results group. Confirm that the query produced the expected results of only the sales during the month of June. At the bottom of the window, you should see "1 of 631" records displayed as shown in Figure 7. Click the **Save** button on the Quick Access Toolbar, and name the query **qryMonthsSales**. Click **OK**. Close the query.

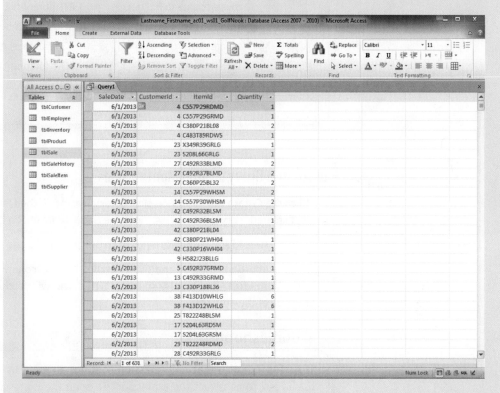

Figure 7   Month's Sales Query in Datasheet view

<table>
<tr><td>**SIDE NOTE**
Available Functions

The available functions in Access are extensive and organized into categories. The categories include Conversion, Date/Time, Financial, Math, and Text. A list of functions is included in the Expression Builder.</td><td>

Intrinsic Functions

An **intrinsic function** is a programmed calculation included in a software application that performs a common process. Because the ProductID field in the tblSaleItem and tblInventory tables is a text field, a text function can be used to exclude the size portion of the product field. The size value in the ProductID field is the last two characters with values such as SM, MD, LG, 02, 04, 06, 28, 30, and 32. The content of a text field can be manipulated using text functions such as MID, RIGHT, and LEFT. The partial product ID is identified by extracting the first 9 characters; LEFT(ProductID, 9). **LEFT(text,[num_chars])** is an intrinsic function that determines the string of characters from the string that is the first argument that makes up the first N characters starting from the left side of the string argument. N is a whole number that is the second argument to the function.</td></tr>
</table>

To Create a Query of Total Month's Sales

a. Click the **Create tab**, and then click **Query Design** in the Queries group. Add the query just created—qryMonthsSales. Close the Show Table dialog box.

b. Add the **ItemId** and **Quantity** fields from the qryMonthsSales query to the current query.

c. Click at the beginning of the Field row in the first column of the design grid. Type SelectItemId: LEFT([. Press End and type],9). This will produce an ItemId that excludes the size of the item sold.

Troubleshooting

If Access indicates that an expression contains an error, use the Expression Builder dialog box to construct the expression. To open the Expression Builder dialog box, right-click the Field column in the design grid.

d. Click the **Totals** button in the Show/Hide group on the Query Tools Design tab on the Ribbon. This adds the Total row to the design grid. In the Quantity column, click the **Group By** entry and select **Sum** from the drop-down list. Click at the beginning of the second column of the Field row in the design grid. Type MonthsSales:.

e. Click the **Run** button to confirm that the query produced the expected results of total sales by inventory item, ignoring size. Observe at the bottom of the window that there are 78 records. Click the **Save** button on the Quick Access Toolbar, name the query qryTotalMonthsSales, and close the query.

Real World Advice   Primary Keys

It is common to embed multiple data values in a primary key. For example, in a Vehicle Identification Number (VIN), there are values that identify the manufacturer, vehicle characteristics, model year, and even at what plant the vehicle was manufactured.

Determining the Starting Inventory

The tblInventory table contains the current inventory for each product. The starting inventory levels are needed in order to determine the popular items. The query of the current inventory is created, and then a query is created to total the quantities of each product. The query design for the current inventory is as shown in Figure 9.

To Create a Query of Current Inventory

a. Click the **Create tab**, and then click **Query Design**. Add the **tblInventory** and **tblProduct** tables. Click **Close** to close the Show Table dialog box.

b. Add the **ProductId**, **ItemId**, **Shelf**, and **Storage** fields from the tblInventory table to the query. Add the **Description** field from the tblProduct table to the query.

c. Click in the Field row of the next empty column in the design grid, and type [shelf] + [storage] as the calculated field. This will compute the total on-hand inventory amount for each inventory item. Click at the beginning of the Field entry of this calculated field. Type InventoryQuantity:.

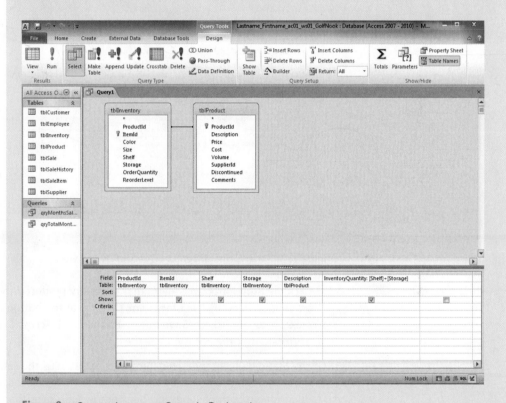

Figure 9   Current Inventory Query in Design view

d. Click the **Run** button to confirm that the query produced the expected results of total amount on hand by inventory item. Observe at the bottom of the window that there are 316 records. Click the **Save** button on the Quick Access Toolbar and name the query qryCurrentInventory. Close the query.

e. Click the **Create tab** and then click **Query Design**. Add the **qryCurrentInventory** query. Close the Show Table dialog box.

f. Add the **ItemId**, **Description**, and **InventoryQuantity** fields from the qryCurrentInventory to the current query.

g. Click at the beginning of the first column in the Field row in the design grid. Type **SelectItemId: LEFT([**. Press [End] and type **],9)**. This will exclude the size of the items in inventory.

h. Click the **Totals** button in the Show/Hide group on the Query Tools Design tab. This adds the Total row to the design grid. In the InventoryQuantity column, click the **Group By** entry and select **Sum** from the drop-down list. Click at the beginning of the Field row for the InventoryQuantity column in the design grid. Type **CurrentInventory:**. The query design should be as shown in Figure 10.

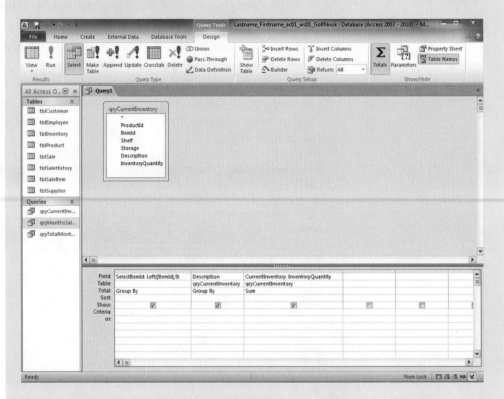

Figure 10   Total Current Inventory Query in Design view

i. Click the **Run** button to confirm that the query produced the expected results of total amount on hand by inventory item. Observe at the bottom of the window that there are 92 records. Click the **Save** button on the Quick Access Toolbar, and name the query **qryTotalCurrentInventory**. Close the query.

The Starting Inventory is the current inventory plus the sales of items since the start of the month of June. The total sales query cannot be used, as that only includes sales during the month of June, and does not include sales that have occurred during the month of July. The query design is as shown in Figure 11.

To Create a Query of Cumulative Sales

a. Click the **Create tab**, and then click **Query Design**. Add the two tables **tblSale** and **tblSaleItem**. The tables are joined on the fields SaleId.

b. Add the **SaleDate** field from the tblSale table, and the **ItemId** and **Quantity** fields from the tblSaleItem table to the query.

c. In the Criteria row in the SaleDate column, type >= 6/1/2013.

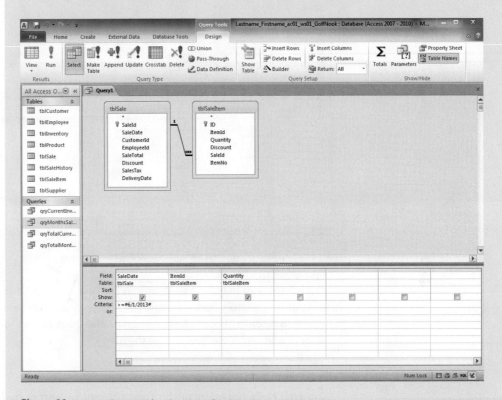

Figure 11 Cumulative Sales Query in Design view

d. Click the **Run** button to confirm that the query produced the expected results of only the sales during the month of June. Observe at the bottom of the window that there are 811 records. Click the **Save** button on the Quick Access Toolbar, and name the query **qryCumulativeSales**. Close the query.

e. Click the **Create tab** and then click **Query Design**. Add the qryCumulativeSales query. Close the Show Table dialog box.

f. Add the **ItemId** and **Quantity** fields from the qryCumulativeSales query to the current query.

g. Click at the beginning of the first column of the Field row in the design grid. Type InventoryId: LEFT([. Press End and type],9). This will exclude the size of the item sold.

h. Click the **Totals** button in the Show/Hide group on the Query Tools Design tab. This adds the Total row to the design grid. In the Quantity column, click the **Group By** entry and select **Sum** from the drop-down list. Click at the beginning of the Field row for the Quantity column in the design grid. Type NumberSoldToDate:. The query design should be as shown in Figure 12.

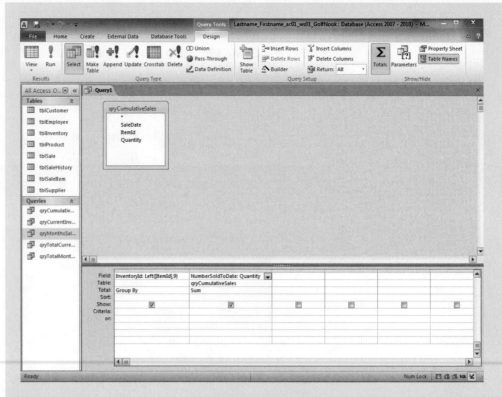

Figure 12 Total Cumulative Sales Query in Design view

i. Click the **Run** button to confirm that the query produced the expected results of total sales by inventory item, ignoring size. Observe at the bottom of the window that there are 78 records. Click the **Save** button on the Quick Access Toolbar, and name the query **qryTotalCumulativeSales**. Close the query.

Now that there is a query of the Total Current Inventory by Item ignoring size, the total Starting Inventory can be determined from the Cumulative Sales by adding the two sums of quantity fields. The query design is as shown in Figure 12.

To Create Query of Starting Inventory

a. Click the **Create tab**, and then click **Query Design**. Add the queries previously created—**qryTotalCumulativeSales** and **qryTotalCurrentInventory**. Close the Show Table dialog box.

b. Add the **SelectItemId**, **Description**, and **CurrentInventory** fields from the qryTotal_Current_Inventory query and then add the **NumberSoldToDate** field from the qryTotalCumulativeSales query to the current query.

c. Click the **InventoryId** field in the qryTotalCumulativeSales query field list and drag it onto the **SelectItemId** field in the qryTotalCurrentInventory query field list in the workspace. This joins the two queries to avoid the multiplier effect.

d. Click in the Field row of the next empty column in the design grid and type in the calculated field **StartingQuantity: [NumberSoldToDate] + [CurrentInventory]**. This will compute the total on-hand inventory amount at the beginning of June 2013.

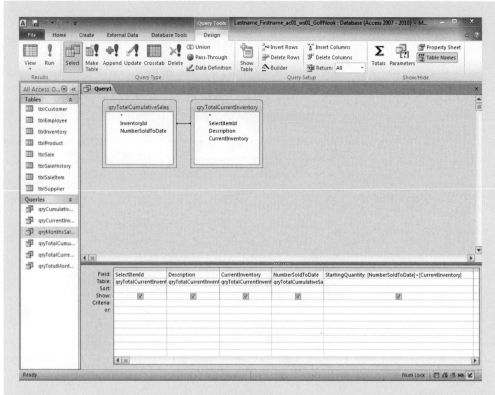

Figure 13   Starting Inventory Query in Design view

e. Click the **Run** button to confirm that the query produced the expected results. Observe at the bottom of the window that there are 78 records. Click the **Save** button on the Quick Access Toolbar, and name the query qryTotalStartingInventory. Close the query.

The two queries—qryTotalStartingInventory and qryTotalMonthsSales—now need to be combined and then exported to Excel for analysis and charting. A calculated field will be included to determine the percentage of starting inventory that was sold in the month of June 2013. The query design is as shown in Figure 14.

Real World Advice   Product Orders

If the database included orders of products that were received since the beginning of June 2013, those quantities would need to be subtracted from the starting inventory amounts.

To Create a Query of Percentage of Starting Inventory Sold in June 2013

a. Click the **Create tab**, and click **Query Design**. Add the queries previously created (**qryTotalMonthsSales** and **qryTotalStartingInventory**). Close the Show Table dialog box.

b. Add the **SelectItemId**, **Description**, and **StartingQuantity** fields from the qryTotal StartingInventory query and the **MonthsSales** from the qryTotalMonthsSales query to the current query.

c. Click the **SelectItemId** field in the field list of the qryTotalStartingInventory query and drag it onto the SelectItemId field in the qryTotalMonthsSales query field list.

d. Click in the Field row of the next empty column in the design grid and type in the calculated field PercentofStartingInventory: [MonthsSales] / [StartingQuantity]. This will compute the percentage of starting inventory that was sold in the month of June 2013. Click in the Sort row for this column in the design grid and select the **Descending** sort option. Click in the **Criteria** row for this column and type > 0.5.

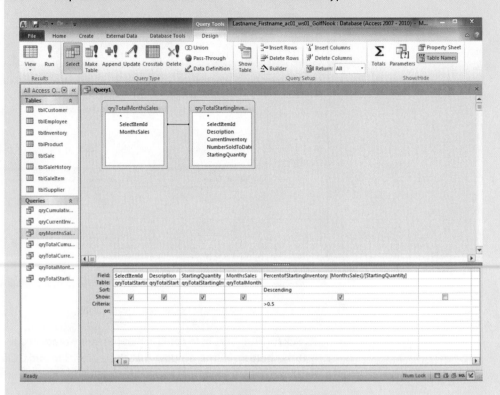

Figure 14   Percent of Starting Inventory Query in Design view

e. Because this is a percent value, the column should be displayed as a percentage. Use the property sheet to format this column as a percentage with two decimal places. Right-click in the **PercentofStartingInventory** column, and click **Properties**. Click the **Format** row, click the drop-down arrow and then click **Percent**. Close the property sheet.

f. Click the **Run** button to confirm that the query produced the expected results. Observe at the bottom of the window that there are 7 records. Click the **Save** button on the Quick Access Toolbar, and name the query qryPercentOfStartingInventory. Close the query.

Exporting Data to Excel for Analysis and Charting

The final query, qryPercentOfStartingInventory, now can be exported to an Excel workbook. The data and formatting can be exported and the Excel workbook opened from Access.

To Export Data to Excel

a. Click the query **qryPercentOfStartingInventory** in the Navigation Pane to select it, if necessary.

b. Click the **External Data tab**, and then click **Excel** in the Export group. The Export-Excel Spreadsheet Wizard window will open. A suggested file name will be in the text box with the default path of the Documents folder.

c. Click the **Export data with formatting and layout** and the **Open the destination file after the export operation is complete** check boxes. This will enable the Open the destination file after the export operation is complete check box. Select this check box.

d. Click **OK**. The Excel program will open with the workbook file named **qryPercentOfStartingInventory** as shown in Figure 15. In Access, click **Close** in the Save Export Steps dialog box.

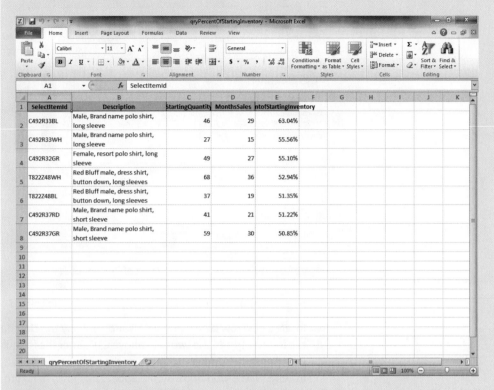

Figure 15 Excel workbook with the exported query data

Analysis and Charting

Notice from examining the Excel data that there is one women's polo shirt, four men's polo shirts, and two Red Bluff dress shirts. For analysis, sort the data by the Description. Then create a chart of the sorted data, selecting the description and the PercentOfStartingInventory. Copy the data to an area below, compute the combined percentages of the three products that are listed twice, and chart the percentages of the products, ignoring color. In this section, you will perform analysis and charting.

To Perform Analysis and Charting

a. Position the mouse pointer between the column headings E and F and double-click to resize column E. Resize other columns as needed. Select the range of cells **A1:E8**. Click the **Home tab** if necessary and then click the **Sort & Filter** button in the Editing group. Click **Custom Sort**. Click **Sort by arrow**, select **Description**, and then click **OK**.

b. Select the range of cells **A1:A8**. Press and hold Ctrl, and with the mouse, select the range of cells **E1:E8**. Click the **Insert tab**, click **Column** in the Charts group, and then select **3D Clustered Column**. Set the Legend option on the Layout tab to **None**.

c. Format the fill color for each of the data point columns to match the color of the product— GR–green, BL–blue, WH–white, RD–red. Click the column. This selects all columns. Click the column to select just this column. Right-click the column, click **Format Data Point**, click **Fill**, and then click **Solid fill**. Select the color from the palette. For the white columns, format the border color of the column to black. Change the chart title to Sales as Percent of Starting Inventory. Position the chart's top-left corner on cell F1 and resize the bottom-right corner to cell O14. The workbook should appear as shown in Figure 16.

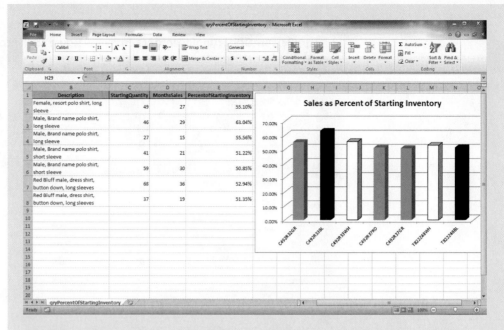

Figure 16   3-D clustered column chart of Percent of Starting Inventory

d. Select the range of cells **A1:E8**. Copy and paste the cells to cell A15.

e. Insert a new row between rows 18 and 19. Copy the Description from B18 to B19. Enter the formula to add the two cells above C19. Enter the formula to add the two cells above D19. Enter the formula to compute the percentage (=MonthsSales/StartingQuantity) in cell E19. The workbook should appear as shown in Figure 17.

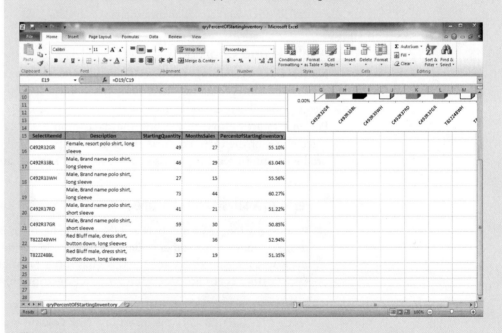

Figure 17   Excel workbook summary analysis

f. Repeat Step e above for the next two pairs of products. Copy the formatting from Row 22 to Row 25.

g. Select the range of cells **B15:B16**. Press and hold Ctrl as you use the mouse to select the following cells and ranges: **B19**, **B22**, **B25**, **E15:E16**, **E19**, **E22**, and **E25**.

h. Click the **Insert tab,** click **Column** in the Charts group, and then select **3D Clustered Column**. Set the Legend option on the Layout tab to **None**. Position the chart's top-left corner on cell A27 and resize the bottom-right corner to cell E43.

i. Save the workbook as Lastname_Firstname_ac01_ws01_Percent_Of_Starting_Inventory, replacing Lastname_Firstname with your actual name. Close Excel. Click **Close** in the Save Export Steps dialog box, and then close Access.

Create a Report of the Problem Solution

With the queries in Access complete and the charting of the data in Excel done, the next task is to create a report for submission and presentation to the store manager. The organization of the report is a cover sheet, table of contents, problem description, background information, problem analysis, recommendation, and supporting documents. The latest draft of the report still needs the cover sheet, table of contents, recommendation, and the charts created in Excel. In this section, you will complete the report creation.

To Complete the Sales Analysis Report

a. Start **Word**. Open **ac01_ws01_Sales_Analysis**. Save the document as Lastname_Firstname_ac01_ws01_Sales_Analysis, replacing Lastname and Firstname with your own name.

b. Click the **Find** button in the Editing group. Type Recommendation to locate and select the Recommendation section.

c. Type in your recommendation to the store manager to send a letter to customers who have not purchased one of the popular products to come in during the current month and purchase them with a 10% discount.

d. Copy the charts created in the Excel workbook of popular products to the chart place-holder in the Sales Analysis report.

e. Position the insertion point at the start of the document using **Ctrl+Home**. Click the **Insert tab**, and then click the **Cover Page** button in the Pages group. Select the **Conservative** style. Type Painted Paradise Resort Golf Nook in the company name placeholder. Type Sales Analysis in the document title placeholder. Type Popular Products in the document subtitle placeholder. Enter your name in the Author place-holder if it is not already there. Set the **Pick the Date** to the current date. Click in the **Abstract**, and then click the **Table Tools Layout tab**. Click the **Delete** button, and then select **Delete Table**. Insert a Next Page section break at the bottom of the cover page.

f. Place the insertion point at the beginning of the next page. Using the References tab on the Ribbon, insert a Table of Contents for the report using Automatic Table 1. Insert a Next Page section break at the bottom of the Table of Contents page. Insert a page number in the footer for the Table of Contents. This page number should not be linked to the previous section (cover page), and should be formatted using roman numerals.

g. Insert the document's file name and page number into the footer from page 3 to the end of the document. This page number should not be linked to the previous section—table of contents page—and should be formatted using decimal numbers. The document footer should appear as shown in Figure 18.

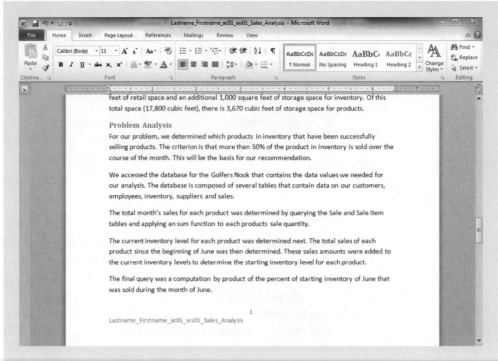

Figure 18   Sales Analysis report with page number and file name in the footer

h. Save and close the document. Close Word.

Develop a Presentation of the Recommended Action

The presentation is based on the report. The presentation is the best opportunity to sell the recommendation to the store manager. The presentation will characteristically be much briefer than the report, which was briefer than the actual analysis in Access and Excel. The Notes pane should be used to have at hand the details of the analysis if questions are asked on how the values were determined. A quality presentation will include anticipated questions in the presentation as appropriate, and answers to other possible questions in the notes. In this section, you will create the presentation.

To Create the Presentation Based on the Sales Analysis Report

a. Start **PowerPoint**. Create a PowerPoint presentation based on the Sales Analysis Report. The presentation should consist of a title slide, a slide introducing the objective, a slide explaining the queries developed, one or more slides with the query results, and a slide with the recommendation from the report.

b. Save the presentation as Lastname_Firstname_ac01_ws01_Sales_Analysis, replacing Lastname and Firstname with your own name.

c. Enter the business name Painted Paradise Resort Golf Nook and your name in the subtitle on the title slide.

d. Enter Popular Products and your name in the footer on all slides except the title slide.

e. Apply the **Civic Theme** to the presentation.

f. Include the two charts created in Excel in the previous activity.

g. Save the presentation and close PowerPoint and Excel.

Plan an Inventory Analysis

The store manager, Susan Williams, has noticed that there appear to be products in the storage area that have not been touched for months. She has also noticed that there seem to be some items that are not available for sale for several days. The store manager has requested that an analysis be done to determine the Optimum Inventory Levels for the store inventory. This would be the combination of display and storage inventory. The Optimum Inventory Level will result in the lowest possible inventory cost while ensuring that items are never out of stock.

Problem Definition

To accomplish these tasks, there are several pieces of information that are needed. One is the actual annual **demand** for each of the products carried in the store over the last year since the store manager was appointed to her position. The actual demand for these products can be used along with the **order cost** and the **holding cost** of an item in inventory to identify the optimum quantity to order and also the optimum inventory level when an item should be reordered. This will result in the minimum cost of maintaining an inventory.

Assuming that there are no unexpected delays in the delivery of an order once the order is placed, this approach will ensure that an item is always available for sale. If this assumption is invalid, then an additional amount is added to the inventory level used for placing an order. This is called a slack amount. This amount will increase the storage cost, but should be offset by the additional revenue that would otherwise be lost by not being able to sell an item when a customer is ready to buy.

The formulas for this analysis have been developed using differential calculus to determine the minimum total inventory cost. As shown in the chart of Inventory Cost in Figure 19, the lowest point on the inventory cost curve is between 250 and 300. For the data used in this example, the monthly demand is 830 units with a cost of $35.00 per unit. The cost to place a single order is $5.50, and the cost to hold a unit in inventory for a month is $0.14. The optimum quantity to order is 255 units. The variables that need to be determined are periodic demand (D_p), the cost of placing a single order (C_o), and the cost of maintaining an item in our inventory, which is called holding cost (H_c). The periodic demand and the period of the holding cost must be the same—e.g., monthly, annually. The periodic demand is obtained from the database of sales over the last month or year.

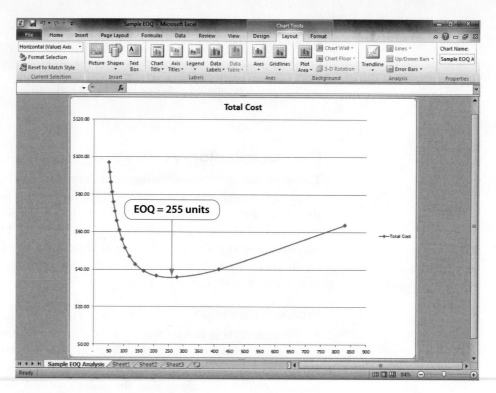

Figure 19   Sample Economic Order Quantity (EOQ) analysis

Using the Sales History table, the annual demand for each item in inventory can be determined. By dividing the annual demand by either 12 or 52, the average monthly or weekly demand can be computed, respectively. The cost of placing a single order is the labor and material cost of creating the order. The cost of the items ordered does not influence the **economic order quantity (EOQ)**. The EOQ is the optimum quantity to order of a product that will result in the minimum total inventory cost. The **reorder point** is the current inventory quantity of a product when a new order should be placed so that the order will arrive when the last product is sold. The holding cost is the item's share of maintaining the entire storage space. Because the item occupies a fixed amount of space—volume—the proportion of total cost is allocated to the item based on the item's proportion of space to the total storable space.

Economic Order Quantity (Q) = Square Root of $[\ (2 \cdot D_p \cdot C_o)\ /\ H_c\ ]$

Reorder Point (L) = Daily demand times the time to receive an order

The information needed from the database is the annual demand for each item in inventory, each item's storage volume, the minimum order amount for the item, and the delay in receiving an ordered item. The other information needed is the cost to maintain the storage spaces and the cost to place an order. This information will come from the store manager. The store manager has confirmed that it takes approximately 15 minutes to place an order using the Internet. The Internet service cost is $200 per month, and is only utilized from an hour before the store opens (9:00 a.m.) to one hour after the store closes (9:00 p.m.). The store manager is paid an annual salary of $45,000, assuming a 40-hour work week. In our case, there are 3,670 cubic feet of available storage space in the store display areas and storage area out of a total volume of 17,800 cubic feet in the store. The cost of this space is the cost of rent and utilities of $1,000 per month, and the labor to organize and clean the store and storage space, which averages $241.50 per week.

With this information, the database query results can be exported to an Excel workbook and the analysis completed. The analysis should be repeated regularly, such as every month, so that changes in demand for products and storage costs are reflected in the inventory levels. In this section, you will create a query of annual demand by product.

To Create a Query of Annual Demand by Product

a. If necessary, open the Access database **Lastname_Firstname_ac01_ws01_Golf_Nook**, and click **Enable Content**. Click the **Create tab**, and then click **Query Design**. Add the **tblSaleHistory** table. Close the Show Table dialog box.

b. Add the **ItemId** and **Quantity** fields to query.

c. Click the **Totals** button in the Show/Hide group on the Query Tools Design tab. This adds the Total row to the design grid. In the Quantity column, click the **Group By** entry, and then select **Sum** from the drop-down list.

d. Click at the beginning of the **Quantity** field, and enter TotalSales: as the new field name.

e. Click at the beginning of the **ItemId** field, and type SelectItem: as the new field name. Type LEFT([. Move to the end of the field and type],9). This will result in the query ignoring the size of the item, which is identified by the last two characters of the ItemId. **Run** the query. There should be 92 records in the query results as shown in Figure 20. Switch back to Design view.

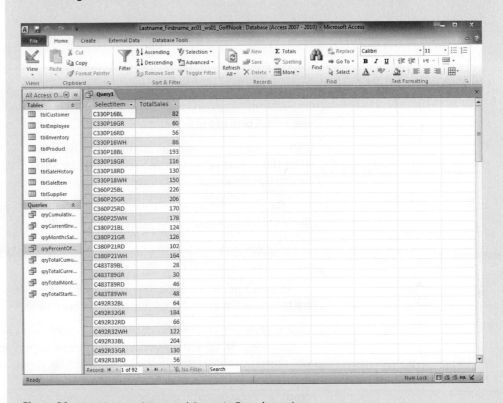

Figure 20   Total Annual Demand Query in Datasheet view

f. Click at the beginning of the next empty Field column in the design grid and type ProductId:LEFT([ItemId],7). This will result in a common field to create a relationship with the tblProduct table.

g. Save the query as qryTotalAnnualDemand. Close the query.

Next, you will create a query of annual sales by product.

To Create a Query of Annual Sales by Product

a. Click the **Create tab**, and then click **Query Design**. Add the **tblProduct** and **tblSupplier** tables. Add the **qryTotalAnnualDemand** query. Close the Show Table dialog box. There should be a relationship between the query and the tblProduct table using ProductId, and a relationship between the tblProduct and tblSupplier tables using SupplierId.

b. Add the **SelectItem** field from the qryTotalAnnualDemand query, the **Description** and **Volume** fields from the tblProduct table, the **TotalSales** field from the qryTotalAnnual-Demand query, and the **OrderDelay** field from the tblSupplier table.

c. Save the query as qryTotalAnnualSales. Close the query.

The query qryTotalAnnualSales now can be exported to an Excel workbook. The data and formatting can be exported and the Excel workbook opened from Access.

To Export Data to Excel for Analysis and Calculations

a. Click **qryTotalAnnualSales** in the Navigation Pane to select the query, if necessary.

b. Click the **External Data tab**, and then click **Excel** in the Export group. The Export-Excel Spreadsheet Wizard window opens. A suggested file name will be in the text box with the default path of the Documents folder.

c. Click the **Export data with formatting and layout** and the **Open the destination file after the export operation is complete** check boxes. This will enable the Open the destination file after the export operation is complete check box. Select this check box.

d. Click **OK**. The Excel program will open with the workbook file named qryTotalAnnualSales. **Close** the Export Wizard.

e. Save the workbook as Lastname_Firstname_ac01_ws01_Optimum_Order_Quantity, replacing Lastname and Firstname with your own name.

f. Select rows 1 through 4 using the row numbers on the left side of the worksheet. Click the **Insert** button in the Cells group to insert four new sheet rows.

g. Click the **File tab**, and then click **Options**. Click **Proofing** in the left pane of the Excel Options window. Click the **AutoCorrect Options** button. Excel's AutoCorrect feature will convert the character sequence (C) to ©. This correction is the first entry in the AutoCorrect dialog box Replace text as you type section. Click the **Replace text as you type** check box so that the check box is not checked and the feature is disabled. Click **OK**. Click **OK** in the Excel Options window.

h. Click cell **A2**. Type Order Cost (C). Press Enter.
Click cell **A4**. Type Holding Cost (h).
Click cell **D1**. Type Manager's Hourly Rate.
Click cell **E1**. Type Internet Access Cost.
Click cell **D3**. Type Rent & Utilities.
Click cell **E3**. Type Monthly Maintenance Cost.
Click cell **F3**. Type Storage Space.
Copy the formatting for these headings from the headings of the query. Click cell **A5** and double-click the **Format Painter** button in the Clipboard group. Click cells **A2**, **A4**, **D1**, **E1**, **D3**, **E3**, and **F3**. Click the **Format Painter** button.

i. Click cell **D2**. Type the formula =45000/52/40 to compute the manager's hourly pay rate. Click cell **E2**. Type the formula =200/30/12/4 to compute the Internet access cost to place an order. This is the Internet access cost per month divided by 30 days for the daily cost. The daily cost is divided by the number of hours there is an employee in the store to access the Internet, which is 12 hours. This hourly rate is then divided by 4 to get the cost of Internet access for the 15 minutes that it takes to place an order. Click cell **B2**. Type the formula =D2/4+E2 to compute the fixed cost to place an order on the Internet.

j. Click cell **D4**. Type the rent and utilities cost for one month which is 1000. Click cell **E4**. Type the formula =241.5*52/12 to compute the monthly inventory maintenance cost. Click cell **F4**. Type the available storage space of 3,670. Click cell **B4**. Type the formula =(D4+E4)/F4 to compute the cost of storage per cubic foot per month. The workbook should now appear as shown in Figure 22. You can check the formulas quickly by switching the display to formulas by holding [Ctrl] + [ ] (left apostrophe). This key combination toggles between displays.

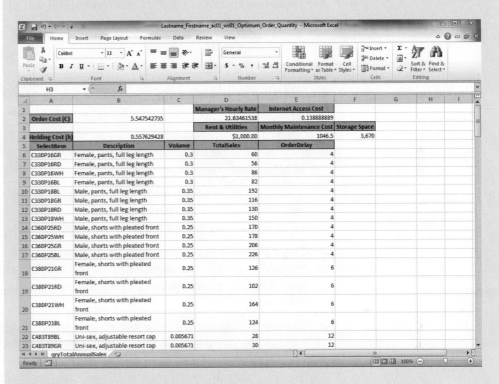

Figure 21   Order cost and holding cost calculations

k. Click cell **F5**. Type EOQ. Click cell **F6**. Type the formula =SQRT(2*D6*B2/(C6*B2*12)). Before this formula can be copied down the column, the cell address of B2 and B4 must be changed to an absolute reference (i.e., B2, B4). Format cell F6 by clicking the Comma style and reducing the number of decimals to zero. Copy cell **F6** to cells **F7:F97**.

l. Click cell **G5**. Type Reorder Point. Resize the column. Click cell **G6**. Type the formula =(D6/365*E6). This formula is the number of items needed in inventory when an order should be placed for the selected product. Copy cell **G6** to cells **G7:G97**.

m. Select the range of cells **A5:F97**. Click the **Name Box** and type EOQ. This creates a named range of the EOQ data and results. Change the Number Format of cell **B2** to **Currency**. Copy this formatting using the Format Painter to cells D2, E2, B4, D4, and E4. Adjust the column widths to Best Fit by double-clicking the column borders in the column heading row.

n. Save the workbook. Enable the AutoCorrect as you type. Click the **File tab** and then click **Options**. Click **Proofing** in the left pane of the Excel Option window. Click the **AutoCorrect Options** button. Click the **Replace text as you type** check box so that the check box is checked and the feature is enabled. Click **OK**. Click **OK** in the Excel Options window.

Analysis Report

With the queries in Access complete and the computations in Excel done, the next task is to create a report for submission and presentation to the store manager. The organization of the report is a cover sheet, table of contents, case background, problem statement, problem definition, information requirements, recommendation, and supporting documents. The latest draft of the report still needs the cover sheet, table of contents, recommendation, and the spreadsheet created in Excel. In this section, you will complete the report.

To Complete the Inventory Analysis Report

a. Start **Word**. Open **ac01_ws01_Inventory_Analysis**. Save the document as Lastname_Firstname_ac01_ws01_Inventory_Analysis, replacing Lastname and Firstname with your own name.

b. Click the **Find** button in the Editing group. Type Recommendation to locate the Recommendation section.

c. Type in your recommendation to the store manager to establish the order amounts for products to be the computed EOQ values, and to use the computed reorder points as the inventory levels that will trigger a new order.

d. **Copy** the spreadsheet created in the Excel workbook of products and their EOQ/Reorder Point values previously created. **Paste** the spreadsheet to the table placeholder in the Supporting Documents section of the Inventory Analysis report. Be sure to delete the placeholder.

e. Position the insertion point at the start of the document using **Ctrl+Home**. Click the **Insert tab**, and then click the **Cover Page** button in the Pages group. Select the **Conservative** style. Click in the company name placeholder. Type Painted Paradise Resort Golf Nook. Type Inventory Analysis in the document title placeholder. Type Optimum Order Quantities in the document subtitle placeholder. Enter your name in the Author place-holder if it is not already there. Set the **Pick the Date** to the current date. Click **Abstract**, and then click the **Table Tools Layout tab**. Click the **Delete** button, and then click **Delete Table**. Insert a Next Page section break at the bottom of the cover page.

f. Place the insertion point at the beginning of the next page. Using the References tab, insert a Table of Contents for the report using Automatic Table 1. Insert a Next Page section break at the bottom of the table of contents page. Insert a page number in the footer for the table of contents. This page number should not be linked to the previous section—cover page—and should be formatted using Roman numerals.

g. Insert the document's file name and page numbers into the footer from page 3 to the end of the document. This page number should not be linked to the previous section—table of contents page—and should be formatted using decimal numbers.

h. Save and close the document. Close Word and Excel.

Analysis Presentation

The presentation is based on the report. The presentation is the best opportunity to sell the recommendation to the store manager. The presentation will characteristically be briefer than the report, which was briefer than the actual analysis in Access and Excel. The Notes pane should be used to have at hand the details of the analysis if questions are asked on how the values were determined. A quality presentation will include anticipated questions in the presentation as appropriate, and answers to other possible questions in the notes. In the next section, you will create the presentation based on the Inventory Analysis report.

To Create the Presentation Based on the Inventory Analysis Report

a. Start **PowerPoint**. Create a PowerPoint presentation based on the Inventory Analysis Report. The presentation should consist of a title slide, a slide introducing the objective, a slide explaining the queries developed, one or more slides with the query results, a slide explaining the computation of the Economic Order Quantity, and a slide with the recommendation from the report.

b. Save the presentation as Lastname_Firstname_ac01_ws01_Inventory_Analysis, replacing Lastname and Firstname with your own name.

c. Enter Optimum Order Quantity and your name in the subtitle on the title slide.

d. Enter your name in the footer on all slides except the title slide.

e. Apply the **Flow Theme** to the presentation.

f. Include the first 15 rows from the spreadsheet created in Excel in the previous activity as a table.

g. Save the presentation. Close PowerPoint and Excel.

Plan a Customer Analysis

The store manager, Susan Williams, believes that the identification of the most popular items can be leveraged to increase the store's sales. Informing customers which items are popular with other customers has the potential to influence their purchases. The store manager has requested that an analysis be done to identify those customers who have not made any purchases in the last month, and those customers who have not purchased one of the popular products identified in the previous analysis. These customers are to be identified so a **Mail Merge** can be used to invite them to a special sales event. If the customer's e-mail address is known, an e-mail with a coupon will be sent. If the customer's e-mail address is not known, a special offer will be mailed. A Mail Merge utility in Microsoft Office combines data from a data source with a form document to produce custom messages.

Problem Definition

In order to determine who has not made a purchase, it is necessary to first determine which customers have made a purchase. Then comparing the list of customers who have made a purchase with a list of all customers will identify those customers who have not made a purchase. The information that needs to be extracted from the database is the customer identifier, name, address, and e-mail address. To determine which customers made a purchase will require information from the tblSale and tblSaleItem tables. If there is an interest in a specific item, the item's identification value is needed. For example, if there is an interest in men's short-sleeve resort polo shirts, add the item identification value of "C492R37" to the query criteria. A parameter query can be used to enter the item identifier at the time the query is run. This eliminates the need to modify the query when the select item changes.

You will now construct the queries by opening the Golf Nook database and enabling the content. The first query will determine the customers who have made a purchase in the previous month. The second query will limit the query results to the first occurrence of a customer so a duplicate message will not be sent to a single customer.

To Create a Query of Customers Who Have Made a Purchase in June 2013

a. If necessary, open the **Lastname_Firstname_ac01_ws01_Golf_Nook** database. Click the **Create tab**, and then click **Query Design**. Add the **tblCustomer**, **tblSale**, and **tblSaleItem** tables. Close the Show Table dialog box.

b. Add the **ID**, **LastName**, **FirstName**, **Address**, **City**, **State**, **ZipCode**, and **E-mailAddress** fields from the tblCustomer table, the **SaleDate** field from the tblSale table, and the **ItemId** field from the tblSaleItem table to the query.

c. Click in the Criteria row of the SaleDate field in the design grid. Type between 6/1/2013 and 6/30/2013. Click in the Criteria row of the ID field. Type >2 to exclude employee and cash sales.

d. **Run** the query to confirm there are 506 records, save the query as qryCustomerPurchasesJune2013, and then close the query.

e. Click the **Create tab**, and then click **Query Design**. Click the **Queries tab**. Add the query qryCustomerPurchasesJune2013. Close the Show Table dialog box.

f. Add the **ID**, **LastName**, **FirstName**, **Address**, **City**, **State**, **ZipCode**, and **E-mailAddress** fields to the query.

g. Click the **Totals** button in the Show/Hide group. Click the **Total row** in the ID field column, and then select **First**.

h. **Run** the query to confirm that there are 117 records, save the query as qryDistinctCustomerPurchasesJune2013, and then close the query.

Next, you will create the query of customers who have not made purchases in June 2013.

To Create a Query of Customers Who Have Not Made a Purchase in June 2013

a. Click the **Create tab**, and then click **Query Wizard**. Select **Find Unmatched Query Wizard**, and then click **OK**. Select the **tblCustomer** table as the source of records for the query results, and then click **Next**.

b. Select **Queries**. Select the **qryDistinctCustomerPurchasesJune2013** query, and then click **Next**. Select the **ID** field in the tblCustomer column and the **FirstOfID** field in the qryDistinctCustomerPurchasesJune2013 column if they are not selected, and then click the <=> between the columns. This establishes the field that will be used to find matching records in the table and the query as shown in Figure 22. Records in the table not matched will be added to the query results. Click **Next**.

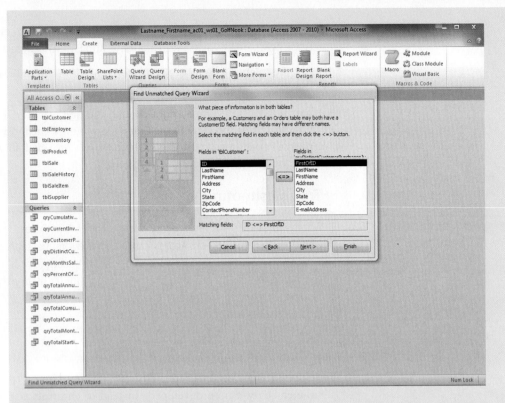

Figure 22　Find Unmatched Query Wizard

c. Move the fields needed for the query results from the left column to the right column. These fields are ID, LastName, FirstName, Address, City State, ZipCode, and E-mailAddress. Click **Next**.

d. Select the field **What would you like to name your query**, type qryCustomers WithoutMatchingPurchaseJune2013, click **Modify the design**, and then click **Finish**. Click in the Criteria row of field ID. Type >2. Run the query. Save and close the query.

An alternative to using the customer's mailing address to create a query of customers who have not made a purchase in June 2013 is to use the customer's e-mail address. This query will only include the LastName, FirstName, and E-mailAddress fields. This will give the Golf Nook the advantage of contacting their customers without incurring the expense of stationery, envelopes, labels, and postage.

To Create a Query of Customers Who Have Not Made a Purchase in June 2013 Listing Their E-mail Addresses

a. Click the **Create tab**, and then click **Query Wizard**. Select **Find Unmatched Query Wizard**, and then click **OK**. Select the **tblCustomer** table as the source of records for the query results, and then click **Next**.

b. Select **Queries**. Select the **qryMonthsSales** query, and then click **Next**. Select the **ID** field in the tblCustomer column and the **CustomerId** field in the qryMonthsSales column, if they are not selected, and then click the <=> between the columns. This establishes the fields that will be used to find matching records in the table and the query. Records in the table not matched will be added to the query results. Click **Next**.

c. Move the fields needed for the query results from the left column to the right column. These fields are ID, LastName, FirstName, and E-mailAddress. Click **Next**.

d. Edit the query name to qryCustomerEmailsWithoutPurchase, and then click **Finish**. The query results will be displayed.

e. Switch to Design view by right-clicking the qryCustomerE-mailsWithoutPurchase tab and clicking Design View. In the Criteria row in the E-mailAddress field, type Is Not Null. This will exclude any customers who have not provided an e-mail address. Click **Run**, save the query, and then close the query.

Troubleshooting

When you are developing a query, form, or report in Access, and an input box appears when you run the object, Access cannot locate a requested value. If you are not using a parameter query, you have mistyped a field. Usually this is in a calculated field that you typed in instead of using the Expression Builder utility that allows you to select fields from existing tables and queries.

To select different products in the future without having to modify the query design, a parameter query can be developed. Instead of entering a specific item identifier in the Criteria row in the design grid, a descriptive term is used that is not a current field name in the field lists. Because Access cannot locate the requested value, an input box opens requesting a value for the term.

To Create a Query of Customers Who Have Made a Popular Product Purchase in June 2013

a. Right-click the **qryCustomerPurchasesJune2013** query in the Navigation Pane and then click **Copy**. Right-click in an empty space of the Navigation Pane, and then click **Paste**. The Paste As dialog box will appear. Edit the query name to be qryCustomerPurchasesOfPopularProducts, and then click **OK**. Next, you will edit the copy of the query to be limited to the Popular Products from the query qryPercentOfStartingInventory.

b. Open the **qryCustomerPurchasesOfPopularProducts** query in Design view. Click in the Field row of the first empty column in the design grid. Type Selected Item: SelectItem. Click in the first Criteria row in this column in the design grid. Type LEFT([ItemID],7). Save the query changes.

c. **Run** the query, input C492R32 in the input box as shown in Figure 23, and then click **OK**. Confirm there are 26 records and all of the records include C492R32 in the ItemId column. Click **Refresh All** in the Records group on the Home tab to run the query again, input T822Z48 in the input box, and then click **OK**. Save and close the query.

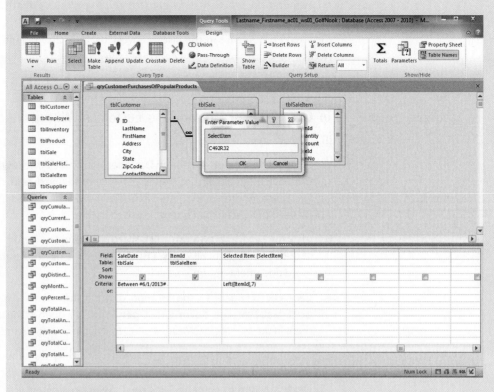

Figure 23 Parameter query input

Next, you will create a query of customers not making a popular product purchase in June 2013.

To Create a Query of Customers Who Have Not Made a Popular Product Purchase in June 2013

a. Click the **Create tab**, and then click **Query Wizard**. Select **Find Unmatched Query Wizard**, and then click **OK**. Select the **tblCustomer** table as the source of records for the query results, and then click **OK**.

b. Click the **Queries** button. Select the **qryCustomerPurchasesOfPopularProducts** query, and then click **Next**. Select the **ID** field in both columns, if they are not selected, and click the <=> between the columns. This establishes the field that will be used to find a matching record in the table and the query. Records in the table not matched will be added to the query results. Click **Next**.

c. Move the fields needed for the query results from the left column to the right column. These fields are ID, LastName, FirstName, Address, City, State, ZipCode, and E-mailAddress. Click **Next**.

d. Edit the query name to be qryCustomersWithoutPurchasesOfPopularProducts, click **Modify the design**, and then click **Finish**. Click in the Criteria row of field ID. Type >2. **Run** the query, input C492R32 in the input box, and then click **OK**. Confirm there are 142 records. Save and close the query.

A merge document will be constructed to produce e-mails to notify the customers who did not make a purchase during June 2013 that they are eligible for a special discount if they make a purchase in the last two weeks of July 2013. This merge can be initiated from Access. A Word document was created for this e-mail message.

To Create E-mail Messages to Customers Who Have Not Made a Purchase in June 2013

a. Open the **tblCustomer** table in Datasheet view. Click the **New (blank) Record** button on the Navigation bar. Press Tab to advance to the next field, then enter your LastName, FirstName, Address, City, State, ZipCode, and E-mailAddress field values. Your record will be used to test the mail merge. Close the table.

b. Click the **External Data tab**. Click **Word Merge** in the Export group. The Microsoft Word Mail Merge Wizard will open. Ensure that the Link your data to an existing Microsoft Word document option is selected.

c. Click **OK**. Navigate to the location of your student data files. Select the file named **ac01_ws01_Merge_Form**. Click **Open**. Word will open in the background with the document in the Mail Merge Wizard at Step 3. Switch the active window to the Word document.

d. In the Word document, click **Previous: Starting document**. Click **Previous: Select document type**. Click the **E-mail messages** option under Select document type. Click **Next: Starting document**. Click **Next: Select recipients**. Click **Next: Write your e-mail message**.

e. Click **Greeting Line** under Write your e-mail message. Click **OK**. Press Enter. Click **Next: Preview your e-mail messages**.

f. Click **Edit Recipient list**. Click the check box in the heading row before the LastName column. This will unselect all of the records. Click the **Find recipient** link in the Mail Merge Recipients dialog box. Type in your last name, click **This field option**, click the drop down arrow, select **LastName**, and then click **Find Next**. Move the Find dialog box so that both LastName and FirstName are visible. If your name is not highlighted, click **Find Next**. Repeat until your name is selected. Click the check box before your last name. Click **OK**.

g. Click **Next: Complete the merge**. Click **Electronic mail**. In the Subject Line: text box, type Special Offer from Golf Nook. Click **OK**.

h. Save the Word e-mail document as Lastname_Firstname_ac01_ws01_E-mail_Merge_Form, replacing Lastname_ Firstname with your actual name. Close Word and then close Access.

i. Open your e-mail account, and open the e-mail message. Save the e-mail message as Lastname_Firstname_ac01_ws01_E-mail_Message, replacing Lastname and Firstname with your own. Exit your e-mail account.

Troubleshooting

If you are using **Outlook**, to save an e-mail message, click the **File tab**, click **Save As**, navigate to the folder in which you are saving the message, type the appropriate file name, and then click **Save**. If you are using another e-mail service, utilize the Help menu to learn to save an e-mail. Note that some e-mail service providers do not have an option to save a message. If that is the case, please see your instructor for directions on how to submit this file.

A merge document will next be constructed to produce letters to notify the customers about the products they are missing out on. Because this merge will be based on a parameter query, the merge must be initiated from Word instead of Access. If a non-parameter query or table is being used to create a mail merge document, the merge can be initiated from Access using the External Data tab as shown previously.

To Create Letters to Customers Who Have Not Made a Purchase in June 2013

a. Start **Word**, and open the **ac01_ws01_Merge_Form** file. Save the document as Lastname_Firstname_ac01_ws01_Merge_Form, replacing Lastname and Firstname with your own name.

b. You will need to select the type of connection that Word will be using to enable the input box for the parameter query. Click the **File tab**. Click **Options**, and then click **Advanced**. Scroll down to the bottom of the dialog box to the **General** category, as shown in Figure 24. Click to turn on the **Confirm file format conversion on open** setting, and then click **OK**.

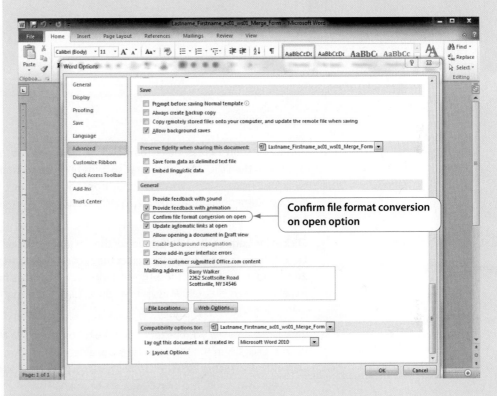

Figure 24   Word Advanced Options dialog box

c. Click the **Mailings tab**. Click **Start Mail Merge** in the Start Mail Merge group. Click **Step by Step Mail Merge Wizard**. Select **Letters** for document type, if necessary, and then click **Next: Starting document**. Select **Use the current document**, if necessary, and then click **Next: Select recipients**.

d. Select **Use an existing list**, if necessary, and then click **Browse**. Navigate to the folder that contains your Lastname_Firstname_ac01_ws01_Golf_Nook database, select it, and then click **Open**.

e. In the **Confirm Data Source** dialog box, click the **Show all** check box. Scroll to the bottom of the dialog box, and then select the **MS Access Databases via DDE(*.mdb, *. mde)** choice, as shown in Figure 25. Click **OK**.

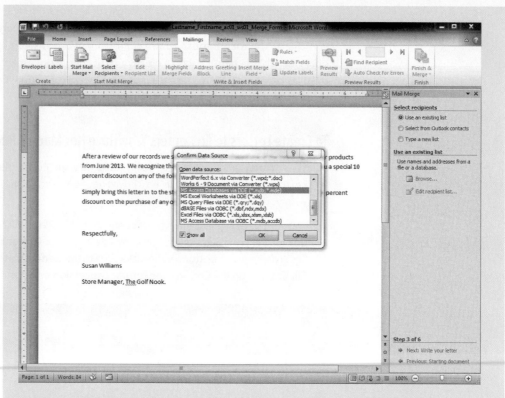

Figure 25   Confirm Data Source dialog box

f.   In the Microsoft Access dialog box, click the **Queries tab**. Scroll down if necessary to locate and then click the query **qryCustomersWithoutPurchasesOfPopularProducts**. Click **OK**. Type C492R32 in the input box, and then click OK. Click anywhere in the Word document window. The Mail Merge Recipients dialog box opens. Click **OK**. Click **Next: Write your letter**.

g.   Click at the beginning of the first line of the document. Click the **Insert tab**, and then click **Date & Time** in the Text group. Select the second date format, **Wednesday, October 5, 2013**, and then click **OK**. Press ⎡Enter⎤ twice. Click **Address block** in the Mail Merge task pane, and then click **OK**. Press ⎡Enter⎤ once. Click **Greeting line** in the Mail Merge task pane. Click **OK**. Press ⎡Enter⎤ once.

h.   Click **Next: Preview your letters**. Click **Next: Complete the Merge**. Click **Edit individual letters**. Click **OK** in the Merge to New Document dialog box. Save the new document as Lastname_Firstname_ac01_ws01_Customer_Letters, replacing Lastname and Firstname with your own name, and then close the document.

i.   Close the Merge Form document without saving changes. Click the **File tab**, click **Options**, click **Advanced**, scroll to the bottom of the Word Options dialog box, turn off the **Confirm file format conversion on open** setting, and then click **OK**. Close Word.

j.   Close the Golf Nook database and close Access.

Next, you will edit the report that will be given to the store manager.

To Complete the Customer Analysis Report

a. Start **Word**. Open **ac01_ws01_Customer_Analysis**. Save the document as Lastname_ Firstname_ac01_ws01_Customer_Analysis, replacing Lastname and Firstname with your own name.

b. Click the **Find** button in the Editing group. Type Recommendation to locate the Recommendation section.

c. Type in the recommendation to the store manager to send a letter to invite each of the customers identified in the query of customers who did not make a purchase in the month of June to come in during the last two weeks of the current month and purchase one of the popular products with a 10% discount.

d. Position the insertion point at the start of the document using **Ctrl+Home**. Click the **Insert tab**, and then click the **Cover Page** button in the Pages group. Select the **Conservative** style. Click in the company name placeholder. Type Painted Paradise Resort Golf Nook. Click in the document subtitle placeholder. Type Customer Analysis. Type Inactive Customers in the document subtitle placeholder. Enter your name in the Author placeholder if it is not already there. Set the **Pick the Date** to the current date. Click **Abstract**, and then click the **Table Tools Layout tab**. Click the **Delete** button, and select **Delete Table**. Insert a Next Page section break at the bottom of the cover page.

e. Place the insertion point at the beginning of the next page. Using the References tab, insert a Table of Contents for the report using Automatic Table 1. Insert a Next Page section break at the bottom of the Table of Contents page. Insert a page number in the footer for the table of contents. This page number should not be linked to the previous section—cover page—and should be formatted using roman numerals.

f. Insert the document's file name and page numbers into the footer from page 3 to the end of the document. This page number should not be linked to the previous section— Table of Contents page—and should be formatted using decimal numbers. Save your document, and then close Word.

Next, create the presentation based on the Customer Analysis report.

To Create the Presentation Based on the Customer Analysis Report

a. Start **PowerPoint**. Create a PowerPoint presentation based on the Customer Analysis Report. The presentation should consist of a title slide, a slide introducing the objective, a slide explaining the queries developed, one or more slides with the query results, and a slide with the recommendation from the report.

b. Save the presentation as Lastname_Firstname_ac01_ws01_Customer_Analysis, replacing Lastname_ Firstname with your actual name.

c. Enter Inactive Customers and your name in the subtitle on the title slide.

d. Enter your name in the footer on all slides except the title slide.

e. Apply the **Paper Theme** to the presentation.

f. Enter the table from the analysis report as a table.

g. Save the presentation. Close **PowerPoint**. Close **Word**.

1. What are some common business problems?

2. How can information solve these problems?

3. Why is it necessary to develop a series of queries to obtain the required information to answer a question?

4. Why would you want to export an Access query to an Excel spreadsheet?

5. What is the purpose of the report document?

6. What is the purpose of the presentation?

Key Terms

ABS( ) 10	Holding cost 21	Order cost 21
Business problem 2	INT( ) 10	Planning steps 2
Data anomalies 3	Intrinsic function 9	Relationship 3
Data redundancy 3	Inventory 2	Reorder point 22
Demand 21	LEFT ( ) 9	ROUND( ) 10
Economic order quantity (EOQ) 22	Mail Merge 27	SQR( ) 10
FIX( ) 10	Normalized 3	SQRT( ) 10

Visual Summary

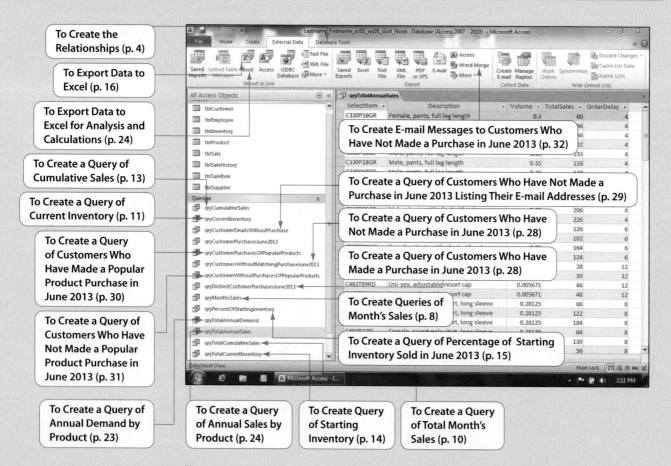

Figure 26 Golf Nook Clothing Store Sales, Inventory, and Customer Analysis Final

Student data files needed:

ac01_ps1_PPRCycles
ac01_ps1_Sales_Analysis
ac01_ps1_Inventory_Analysis
ac01_ps1_Merge_Form
ac01_ps1_Customer_Analysis

You will save your files as:

Lastname_Firstname_ac01_ps1_PPRCycles
Lastname_Firstname_ac01_ps1_Percent_Of_Sales
Lastname_Firstname_ac01_ps1_Sales_Analysis (Word)
Lastname_Firstname_ac01_ps1_Sales_Analysis (PowerPoint)
Lastname_Firstname_ac01_ps1_Average_Monthly_Sales
Lastname_Firstname_ac01_ps1_Inventory_Analysis (Word)
Lastname_Firstname_ac01_ps1_Inventory_Analysis (PowerPoint)
Lastname_Firstname_ac01_ps1_Customer_Letters
Lastname_Firstname_ac01_ps1_Customer_E-mails
Lastname_Firstname_ac01_ps1_Customer_E-mails.msg
Lastname_Firstname_ac01_ps1_Customer_Analysis (Word)
Lastname_Firstname_ac01_ps1_Customer_Analysis (PowerPoint)

Painted Paradise Resort Cycle Sales and Rentals

At Painted Paradise Resort (PPR) Cycles shop, Andrew Fleming serves as the store manager, Catherine Smith serves as the assistant store manager, and William Port is a full-time sales associate. There are six part-time employees and two additional full-time mechanics. Part-time employees work one or more 4-hour shifts per week. The mechanics are responsible for the maintenance of the rental bikes, and assembly and fitting of bicycles sold in the shop. The shop carries bicycles from two manufacturers, Trek and Specialized. Other suppliers include Nike and Adidas. The sales are collected during the day and added to the sales table in the database. The store is open from 9 a.m. to 6 p.m. daily. Information on customers is gathered at the time of the sales by encouraging customers to participate in the company rewards program. The display section of the cycle store has approximately 800 square feet of retail space and an additional 800 square feet of storage space for inventory, store manager's office, and mechanics' area. Of this total space—14,400 cubic feet—there are 2,640 cubic feet of storage space for products.

Andrew Fleming has requested that an analysis be done to identify ways to increase sales of the most popular items that are being purchased on a monthly basis. An item is considered "popular" when over half of the in-store inventory is sold during one month and has not been previously placed on sale due to sales inactivity. You will develop the requested analysis using the available information in an Access database and the capabilities of an Excel workbook. You will then use a Word document to develop a written report that will clearly describe the problem, relevant background information, data sources that were selected from the database and why they were selected, the analysis process, how the queries of the database were developed and imported to Excel, how the data were manipulated in Excel, and your conclusions and recommendations. You will also use the report information to create a PowerPoint presentation for the store manager.

A database for PPR Cycles has been provided that contains the data values needed for this analysis. The database is composed of several tables that contain data on customers, employees, inventory, suppliers, sales, and rentals.

a. Open **ac01_ps1_PPRCycles**, and save it as Lastname_Firstname_ac01_ps1_PPRCycles, replacing Lastname_Firstname with your own name.

b. Create the relationships among the tables in the database. The foreign keys in the tblSale and tblRental tables will need to have the field size changed from Number (Double) to Number (Long Integer) before the relationships can be created successfully.

Table With Primary Key	Table With Foreign Key	Apply Referential Integrity
tblCustomer	tblSale	Yes
tblEmployee	tblSale	Yes
tblCustomer	tblRental	Yes
tblEmployee	tblRental	Yes
tblSale	tblSaleItem	Yes
tblInventory	tblSaleItem	No
tblProduct	tblInventory	Yes
tblSupplier	tblProduct	Yes
tblProduct	tblSaleHistory	No

Figure 27   Table relationships in the Painted Paradise Resort Cycles database

c. Save the relationships, and close the Relationships window.

d. Create the following queries for products.

- Create a query in Design view using the tblSale and tblSaleItem tables, selecting the **SaleDate**, **Quantity**, and **InventoryId** fields. Set a criterion of dates for May 2014. Save the query as qryMay2014Sales. Close the query.

- Create a query in Design view using the qryMay2014Sales query created previously. The product identification value is the first seven characters of the InventoryId field. Add the **Quantity** field and the first seven characters of the **InventoryId** field to the design grid. Add the column name ProductId. Total the Quantity amount for each product, and name the Quantity column TotalSales. Save the query as qryTotalMay2014Sales.

- Create a query in Design view using the tblInventory and tblProduct tables. Select the **ProductId**, **Description**, and **Quantity** fields. Show the Total row, and apply Sum to the Quantity field. Add a Column name of CurrentInventory to the Quantity field. Save the query as qryCurrentInventory.

- Create a query in Design view using the tblSale and tblSaleItem tables. Add the **SaleDate**, **Quantity**, and **InventoryId** fields to the design grid. Edit the InventoryId column to extract only the first seven characters. Add a new column named **ProductId**. Set a criterion of sale dates since May 1, 2014. Save the query as qryCumulativeSales.

- Create a query in Design view using the qryCumulativeSales created previously. Add the **Quantity** and **ProductId** fields to the design grid. Sum the Quantity amount for each product, and then rename the field TotalSales. Save the query as qryTotalCumulativeSales.

- Create a query in Design view using the qryTotalCumulativeSales and qryCurrentInventory queries created previously. Add the **ProductId** and **Description** fields to the design grid. Add a calculated field named StartingInventory that adds the CurrentInventory and TotalSales fields. Save the query as qryStartingInventoryMay2014.

- Create a query in Design view using the qryTotalMay2014Sales and qryStartingInventory queries created previously. Add the **ProductId**, **Description**, **StartingInventory**, and **TotalSales** fields to the design grid. Add a calculated field named PercentOfSales that computes the percentage of starting inventory that has been sold in the month of May 2014. Set a criterion of over 50%. Save the query as qryPercentOfSales.

e. Select the **qryPercentOfSales** query in the Navigation Pane. Export the query with formatting and layout to an Excel spreadsheet using the External Data tab. Name the Excel file Lastname_Firstname_ac01_ps1_Percent_Of_Sales. Open the workbook after the export operation is complete.

f. Create a chart of the popular items. Create a chart of the different product groups. Save the workbook.

g. Start **Word**. Open **ac01_ps1_Sales_Analysis**, and save it as Lastname_Firstname_ac01_ps1_Sales_Analysis, replacing Lastname_Firstname with your own name. Make the following changes to the file.

- Use Find to locate the Recommendation heading.
- Type in the recommendation to the store manager to send a letter to customers who have not purchased a bicycle in the month of May, asking them to consider one of the most popular models and offering a 10% discount.
- Copy the charts created in the Excel Lastname_Firstname_ac01_ps1_Percent_Of_Sales workbook of popular products to the chart placeholder in the Sales Analysis report.
- Copy the query results from the qryPercentOfSales in Access to the supporting documents.
- Add a Cover Page to the report using the **Conservative** style. Type Painted Paradise Resort Cycles in the company name placeholder. Type Sales Analysis in the document title placeholder. Type Popular Products in the document subtitle placeholder. Enter your name in the Author placeholder if it is not already there. Set the **Pick the Date** to the current date. Click **Abstract**, and then click the **Table Tools Layout tab**. Click the **Delete** button, and then select **Delete Table**. Insert a Next page section break.
- Insert a Table of Contents for the report using Automatic Table 1. Insert a Next Page section break at the bottom of the table of contents page. Insert a page number in the footer for the table of contents. This page number should not be linked to the previous section—cover page—and should be formatted using Roman numerals.
- Insert the document's file name and page number into the footers from page 3 to the end of the document. This page number should not be linked to the previous section—table of contents page—and should be formatted using decimal numbers.

h. Save and close the document. Close Word.

i. Start **PowerPoint**. Save a new presentation as Lastname_Firstname_ac01_ps1_Sales_Analysis, replacing Lastname and Firstname with your own name. The final presentation should consist of a title slide, a slide introducing the objective, a slide explaining the queries developed, one or more slides with the query results, and a slide with the recommendation from the report. Make the following changes to the presentation.

- Enter Popular Products and your name in the subtitle on the title slide.
- Enter your name in the footer on all slides except the title slide.
- Apply the **Trek Theme** to the presentation.
- Enter the table from the analysis report as a table.

j. Save and close the presentation and spreadsheet. Exit PowerPoint, and then exit Excel.

In the next steps, an inventory analysis needs to be added. The store manager, Andrew Fleming, has requested that an analysis be done to determine the Optimum Inventory Levels for the store inventory. This would be the combination of display and storage inventory. The Optimum Inventory Level will result in the lowest possible inventory cost while ensuring that items are never out of stock.

The information needed from the database is the average monthly demand for each item in inventory, and each item's storage volume. The other information needed is the cost to maintain the storage spaces and the cost to place an order. This information will come from the store manager. The store manager has confirmed that it takes approximately 20 minutes to place an order using the Internet. The Internet service cost is $250 per month. The store manager is paid an annual salary of $47,800, assuming a 40-hour work week. In our case, there are 2,640 cubic feet of available storage space in the store display areas and in the storage area out of a total volume of 14,400 cubic feet in the store. The cost of this space is the cost of rent and utilities of $1,000 per month and the labor to organize and clean the store and storage space, which averages $119.50 per week. You will now create queries needed for the analysis.

k. Navigate to or reopen the **Lastname_Firstname_ ac01_ps1_PPRCycles** database. Create the following queries to determine average monthly demand and item storage volume.

- Create a query to include the ProductID, Description, Volume fields in the tblProduct, and Quantity field in the tblSaleHistory. Rename the Quantity field YTDSales, and Sum the quantity. Name the query qryYTDAnnualSales.

- Create a query based on the previous qryYTDAnnualSales query to compute the average monthly demand. The results should return 62 records. Name the query qryAverageMonthlySales.

l. Export—including data and formatting—the average monthly demand query to an Excel workbook file named Lastname_Firstname_ac01_ps1_Average_Monthly_Sales. Make the following changes to this Excel file.

- In the first four rows, add computations for Order Costs and Holding Cost. Format currency values appropriately.

- Add columns for annual demand, the EOQ computation, and the reorder point using Average Monthly Demand, Order Costs, Holding Costs, Volume, and DeliveryDelay.

m. Save the Excel workbook. Exit Excel.

n. Start **Word**. Open **ac01_ps1_Inventory_Analysis**, and save it as Lastname_Firstname_ ac01_ps1_Inventory_Analysis. Make the following changes to the file.

- Type in the recommendation to the store manager to establish the order amounts for each product to be the computed EOQ values under the Recommendation heading.

- Add a Cover Page to the report using a style of your choice. Update the company name, the document title, and the document subtitle placeholders. Enter your name in the Author placeholder. Set the current date. **Delete** the table. Insert a section break.

- Insert a Table of Contents for the report with a page number in the footer.

- Insert the document's file name and page number into the footers from page 3 to the end of the document.

o. Save and close the document. Exit Word.

p. Start **PowerPoint**. Save the presentation as Lastname_Firstname_ac01_ps1_Inventory_Analysis. In the final form, you will create a PowerPoint presentation based on the Inventory Analysis report. The presentation should consist of a title slide, a slide introducing the objective, a slide explaining the queries developed, one or more slides with the query results, and a slide with the recommendation from the report. Make the following changes to the presentation.

- Enter Optimum Order Quantity and your name in the subtitle on the title slide.

- Enter your name in the footer on all slides except the title slide.

- Apply the **Trek Theme** to the presentation.

- Include the tables from the analysis report as tables.

q. Save and close the presentation. Exit PowerPoint.

The store manager believes the customers who rent bicycles are excellent potential customers to purchase a bicycle. These customers could be contacted with a special offer to encourage bicycle sales. The store manager, Andrew Fleming, has requested that an analysis be done to identify the customers who have rented a bicycle but not purchased a bicycle in the last month. These customers are to be identified so a mail merge can be used to invite these customers to a special sales event. If the customer's e-mail address is known, an e-mail with a coupon will be sent. If the customer's e-mail address is not known, a special offer will be mailed. In the next steps, you will create queries to determine customers who have rented, customers who have purchased, and those customers who have rented but not purchased.

r. Navigate to or reopen **Lastname_Firstname_ ac01_ps1_PPRCycles** database.

s. Open the **tblCustomer** table in Datasheet view. Click **New (blank) Record** button on the Navigation bar. Type in your LastName, FirstName, Address, City, State, ZipCode, and E-mailAddress field values. Save and close the table. Open the **tblRental** table in Datasheet view. Click **New (blank) Record** button on the Navigation bar. Type in the following values for the new record's fields—Date: 5/31/2013, Type: Half, TimeOut: 1:00 PM, TimeIn: 5:00 PM, Employee: 7, Customer: 129, BikeId: B128CR3H17003515, Rental: 12.5, SalesTax: 0.88. Your record will be used to test the mail merge.

t. Save and close the table. Next, make the following queries.

- Create a query of the tblCustomer and tblRental tables, including mailing address and e-mail address, listing each customer once. Name the query qryCustomerRentals.

- Create a query of the tblCustomer and tblSale tables, including mailing address and e-mail address, listing each customer once. Name the query qryCustomerSales.

- Create a query of those customers who have rented a bicycle, but not purchased a bicycle. Include the customer's mailing address and e-mail address. Name the query qryCustomerRentalsWithoutBikeSale.

- Create a query of the customers without an e-mail address, and create a traditional mail merge letter using the file **ac01_ps1_Merge_Form**, offering a 10% discount on a bicycle purchase within the next two weeks. Name the query qryMailMergeCustomersNoEmail. Name the document file Lastname_Firstname_ac01_ps1_Customer_Letters.

- Create a query of those customers not included in the previous query, and create an e-mail mail merge document using the file **ac01_ps1_Merge_Form**, offering a 10% discount on a bicycle purchase within the next month. Name the query qryMailMergeCustomersEmails. Name the document file Lastname_Firstname_ac01_ps1_Customer_Emails.

  Now, you can complete the Customer Analysis report in the next steps.

u. Start **Word**. Open **ac01_ps1_Customer_Analysis**, and save it as Lastname_Firstname_ac01_ps1_Customer_Analysis. Make the following changes to the file.

- Type in the recommendation to the store manager to send a letter or e-mail as appropriate to each of the customers identified in the query of customers who have not made a purchase, but have rented a bicycle in the month of May, to come in during the next two weeks and purchase a bicycle with a 10% discount under the Recommendation heading.

- Add a Cover Page to the report. Update the company name, the document title, and the document subtitle placeholders.

- Enter your name in the Author placeholder. Set the date to the current date. Delete the table.

- Insert a table of contents for the report with a page number in the footer. Insert the document's file name and page number into the footers from page 3 to the end of the document.

v. Save and close the document. Exit Word.

w. Start **PowerPoint**. Save the presentation as Lastname_Firstname_ac01_ps1_Customer_Analysis. In the final form, you will create a PowerPoint presentation based upon the Customer Analysis report. The presentation should consist of a title slide, a slide introducing the objective, a slide explaining the queries developed, one or more slides with the query results, and a slide with the recommendation from the report. Make the following changes to the presentation.

- Enter Inactive Customers and your name in the subtitle on the title slide.

- Enter your name in the footer on all slides except the title slide.

- Apply the **Trek Theme** to the presentation.

- Include the table from the analysis report as a table.

x. Save and close the presentation. Exit PowerPoint, and then exit Access.

Objectives

1. Build a decision support system   p. 45

2. Perform a financial analysis   p. 45

3. Build a database   p. 51

4. Work with customer data to create queries   p. 56

5. Request additional customer data to develop a marketing mailer   p. 59

6. Identify the target market   p. 63

7. Develop a SWOT analysis   p. 69

8. Analyze an industry using Porter's Five Forces model   p. 72

9. Develop the components of the business plan   p. 78

Solving Business Problems

PREPARE CASE

My Sparkles: Developing a Business Plan, Creating a Financial Analysis, and Managing Customers and Inventory

My Sparkles, a new company opened by Laura Schmidt, sells and distributes hand-made and custom-made jewelry. The company is currently operated out of the owner's home. My Sparkles is experiencing tremendous growth and Laura has realized the need to secure a storefront, which will require her to apply for a bank loan. Additionally, she wants to be able to respond quickly to inventory needs not only

Elena Elisseeva / Shutterstock.com

to maximize revenues and profits, but to ensure that she can afford to pay off the loan. By opening a storefront, she understands the need to broaden her customer base. Her existing customer base has been built on customer referrals. To grow her company and reward her current customers for their loyalty and referrals, she wants to develop a customer reward program and marketing plan. Because of your technical expertise, Laura has hired you as an intern to develop a business plan that will be used when applying for a bank loan, create a financial analysis of current and forecasted sales trends, and to help manage current and prospective customers. If Laura is unable to obtain a bank loan, she will need to present her plan to a prospective investor. To prepare Laura for all possible financing situations, she will also need you to create an analysis using Porter's Five Forces model and a SWOT analysis.

Student data files needed for this workshop:

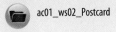

- ac01_ws02_Financials
- ac01_ws02_Proforma
- ac01_ws02_Logo
- ac01_ws02_Customers
- ac01_ws02_Postcard
- ac01_ws02_Persona

- ac01_ws02_FemalePersona
- ac01_ws02_Analysis
- ac01_ws02_LoyaltyFlyer
- ac01_ws02_Jewelry
- ac01_ws02_BusinessPlan
- ac01_ws02_OperationsPlan

You will save your files as:

- Lastname_Firstname_ac01_ws02_Financials
- Lastname_Firstname_ac01_ws02_MySparkles
- Lastname_Firstname_ac01_ws02_Postcard
- Lastname_Firstname_ac01_ws02_PostcardMerged
- Lastname_Firstname_ac01_ws02_Persona
- Lastname_Firstname_ac01_ws02_Analysis

- Lastname_Firstname_ac01_ws02_LoyaltyFlyer
- Lastname_Firstname_ac01_ws02_BusinessPlan

Developing a Business Plan

Many times a new business will have to use a decision support system to determine the feasibility of a business loan that will cover startup costs. **Startup costs** are fixed costs associated with starting a business. These costs are often non-reoccurring costs such as legal fees, advertising fees, promotional activity fees, and employee training. It can be challenging for new businesses to obtain a loan because the business has not established a proven track record.

The owner, Laura Schmitt, has asked you to help compile a business plan to communicate to the bank that she is worthy of being approved for a loan. A **business plan** is a formal statement that summarizes forecasted—usually one to three years—operational and financial objectives and explains how they will be achieved. Business plans can be created for internal or external audiences. A business plan for external audiences, such as lenders or prospective investors, outlines the past, present, and forecasted performance of the organization. Additionally, it contains a pro-forma balance sheet, income statement, and cash flow statement to illustrate how the financing being sought will affect the organization's financial situation.

A pro-forma balance sheet is similar to a regular balance sheet; however, it includes a summary of how the business is expected to perform in the future. A **balance sheet** illustrates the outflow and inflow of cash over a certain period of time. One side shows the organization's assets and liabilities, while the other side shows how they are financed. The two sides must match in value, or "balance." A **pro-forma balance sheet** displays similar information, but also illustrates events that have happened during the period of time in which the balance sheet has been created. This permits people within the organization to identify trends more easily and predict how much cash they will have at a specific period in time. The **income statement**—also referred to in business as a statement of profit and loss—itemizes past revenues and expenses that caused the current profit or loss, and indicates what may be done to improve the results. A **cash flow statement**—also known as statement of cash flows or funds flow statement—is a financial statement that indicates how changes in balance sheet accounts and revenue affect cash and cash equivalents, and then breaks the analysis down to operating, investing, and financing activities. Simply put, the cash flow statement shows the organization's **liquidity** or ability to quickly convert assets, such as money market accounts, bonds, or Treasury bills, to cash.

Laura has been selling jewelry out of her home for the past year. The business began as a hobby and once her designs were worn by both men and women, sales doubled within three months. She has kept records of sales and expenses, but some methods of record-keeping have not been efficient. For example, she has been typing the results of calculations into the cells of an Excel workbook instead of using functions and formulas within Excel to automatically calculate results. As Laura's intern, you will modify her existing income statement and create the pro-forma balance sheet and cash flow statement which will be included in your final business plan.

CONSIDER THIS | **How Do You Save Money?**

Have you ever saved money to purchase something you really wanted? Maybe concert tickets or even a car? How "liquid" are you? Do you place your money in a savings account? Do you purchase stocks or savings bonds? Do you open a certificate of deposit (CD) account? Which of these options makes you more liquid? If you want to have access to your cash quickly, you need to consider how long it will take you to retrieve it. For example, CDs require you to keep your money in the account for a specific period of time, such as six months or a year.

Building a Decision Support System

A **decision support system** (DSS) is an information system that supports managerial decision-making activities by representing a problem, either mathematically or symbolically, that a manager needs to solve. For example, the creator of a DSS can use data that are located in a spreadsheet or database, prepare a mathematical model using the data, and solve or analyze this model using problem-specific methods. Because Excel has standard built-in functions as well as many financial and statistical functions, many types of problems—such as accounting, financial, and operational—can be modeled in an Excel spreadsheet. An **Excel model** includes a series of equations, input factors, parameters, and variables that are used to solve the problem at hand. It is important to note that DSSs are not meant to replace managers, but to augment their decision-making capabilities by presenting information in a way that calls attention to important trends and thresholds.

DSSs help managers model and solve business problems mainly through the use of what-if analysis. **What-if analysis** is the process of changing the values in certain cells to see how those changes will affect the outcome of formulas or functions within the worksheet. Because data may rapidly change and be difficult to specify in advance, what-if analysis is a practical tool to use when testing multiple variables.

CONSIDER THIS | **Creating Your Own What-If Analysis**

Think about the questions you have asked yourself that begin with the words "what if." Perhaps you have wondered what grade you would earn in a class if you obtained a certain score on a final exam. You could build a DSS in Excel that will help you answer this question. What data would you need to include? How would you change the model for courses that use weighted average versus straight percentage?

It is important to remember that:

1. DSSs are explicitly designed to simplify decision-making processes.
2. DSSs should support rather than automate decision making.
3. DSSs should be able to rapidly respond to the changing needs of decision makers.
4. DSSs should be used to differentiate between critical assumptions or compare alternative models.

Perform a Financial Analysis

Laura needs to determine how My Sparkles has been performing over the past year. A pro-forma balance sheet, income statement, and cash flow statement need to be created to illustrate how the financing being sought will affect the organization's financial situation. Laura has been keeping accurate records in Excel and Word; however, you need to import some data from Word into Excel and then format her Excel workbook so it is more efficient through the use of formulas and functions. Additionally, the workbook needs to be formatted professionally so banks and prospective investors will take her seriously as a businesswoman.

Real World Advice   Present Yourself in the Best Light

If you need to obtain financing from a lender, every minute detail matters. The bank will look at how you present yourself both on paper and in person. Thus, it is imperative that you and your paperwork look professional. Furthermore, your calculations must be accurate. If an error is found on your pro-forma balance sheet, income statement, or cash flow statement, a lender can doubt your ability both as an entrepreneur and when managing your finances. Always remember to pay attention to every detail, double-check your work, and be confident in your ability.

The My Sparkles workbook contains the data values needed for analysis. The workbook is composed of several worksheets, including a pro-forma balance sheet, income statement, and cash flow statement. Laura has already entered some data into Excel, but not all of the data needed to create the financial documents.

In business, pro-forma financial statements are prepared in advance of a planned activity, such as a merger or acquisition, a new capital investment, or a change in capital structure such as incurrence of new debt—such as a loan—or the provision of equity. Laura has given you an Excel workbook that includes a worksheet named Pro-forma Balance Sheet. She has added the heading, subheading, and some formatting for you. Because she has already found a location for her business, she has included the amounts she would pay to maintain the location. Because she has entered the pro-forma data into a Word document, you will need to import the data into the workbook and then add formulas to calculate totals. She has saved the data as a text file to make it easier for you to import.

By reporting income and expenses over the past year, the income statement should help My Sparkles investors and creditors evaluate the past financial performance of the organization, predict future performance, and measure the ability of generating future cash flows. Laura created an income statement in the workbook; however, she did not use functions to calculate totals nor did she name the totals cells, which will be referenced on the cash flow statement worksheet.

The cash flow statement documents the flow of cash in and out of the business. As an analytical tool, the cash flow statement is useful in determining the short-term capability of a company, particularly its ability to pay bills. Potential lenders want a clear picture of Laura's ability to repay a loan. If Laura is not able to obtain a bank loan, she will have to seek out an investor. Potential investors will need to judge whether the company is financially sound. Neither potential lenders nor investors will fund Laura's business if they do not believe she can repay the loan. Laura created a cash flow statement in the workbook; however, she did not use functions to calculate totals nor did she reference data already included on the income statement.

In addition to creating financial reports, Laura also needs to modify the existing product listing along with retail prices for each item. She will need you to calculate the forecasted sales totals based on her projections for the second year in business. These totals will be added to your cash flow projection for next year. Laura knows that opening a store will increase expenses and forecasts that depreciation will increase by 250 percent, accounts payable will increase by 300 percent, accrued income taxes will increase by 1,000 percent, accounts receivable will increase by 3,000 percent, and equipment will increase by 500 percent; in addition, the increase in inventory will be the difference between the forecasted 2014 value and the ending inventory for 2013. Because of this, she believes that by borrowing $50,000, she will be able to purchase a retail location, additional equipment, and raw materials needed for creating more jewelry.

In this section, you will finalize the pro-forma balance sheet, income statement, and cash flow statement, which will be included in the final business plan. In addition to importing the pro-forma data and creating calculations, you will also need to apply formatting to ensure that the worksheets are visually appealing and professional.

Quick Reference — Pro-forma Balance Sheet Items

Pro-forma balance sheets can vary based on who is actually creating it. The main categories include assets and liabilities. An **asset** is an object you own that holds value such as cash, stock, inventory, property rights, and goodwill. A **liability** is an item that someone is legally responsible for such as an obligation, responsibility, or debt.

Item	Description
Current Assets	Can either be converted to cash or used to pay current liabilities within 12 months. Typical current assets include cash and cash equivalents, short-term investments, accounts receivable, inventory, and the amount of prepaid liabilities, which will be paid within a year. Current assets are also classified as liquid assets.
Fixed Assets	Cannot easily be converted to cash and in the accounting industry, these are classified as property, plant, and equipment. Typical fixed assets include buildings, land, equipment, furniture, and fixtures.
Current Liabilities	Often categorized as all liabilities of the business that are to be paid in cash within the fiscal year or the operating cycle of a given firm, whichever period is longer. Accounts payable are due within 30 days, and are paid within 30 days. Some situations do cause these to run past 30 or 60 days.
Long-Term Liabilities	Categorized as liabilities with a future value greater than one year, such as mortgage loans and other bank loans that mature longer than one year.

Figure 1   Items included on a pro-forma balance sheet

To Create the Pro-forma Balance Sheet, Income Statement, and Cash Flow Statement

a. Click the **Start** button, and then select **Excel 2010**.

b. Click the **File tab**, click **Open**, locate and select **ac01_ws02_Financials**, and then click **Open**.

c. Browse to where you are storing your student files. In the File name box, type Lastname_ Firstname_ac01_ws02_Financials, replacing Lastname_Firstname with your actual name and then click **Save**.

d. Click the **Pro-forma Balance Sheet worksheet tab**, and then click cell **A7**. Import the data from **ac01_ws02_Proforma** into the worksheet. Use a function to calculate the totals in cells B13, B19, B20, B27, B31, and B32. Bold and underline the text in each section heading, bold the text in each section subheading, and then italicize the text in each cell that has the word Total in it. Increase the indent in all items under each subheading that do not have any other formatting applied. Apply the Accounting format to the first number under each subheading and each number in the Total sections. Apply Comma formatting to all other numbers and then remove all decimals in column B. Resize columns A and B so all data are visible. In cells B20 and B32, apply a Top and Double Bottom Border, and then apply conditional formatting so negative numbers will display as red text. Select ranges **A7:G7** and **A21:G21**, and then apply the **Purple, Accent 4, Lighter 80%** color fill.

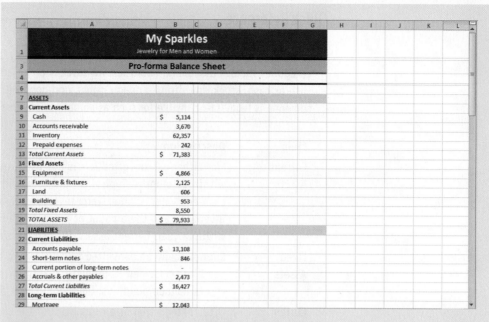

Figure 2   Pro-forma Balance Sheet worksheet

e. Click the **Income Statement worksheet tab**. Assign an appropriate name to cells D9, D17, D19, D21, D25, D29, D31, D36, and D38. Use a formula or function to calculate the totals in cells D9, D17, D19, D21, D29, D31, D36, and D38; and then apply conditional formatting so negative numbers will display as red text. In cell D38, apply conditional formatting so a positive number will display as Green Fill with Dark Green Text. Bold and underline the text in A6, A11, A23, and A33. Bold the text in the totals rows, and then increase the indent. Apply the Accounting format to the first number in each section and each cell that contains subtotals or totals, apply Comma formatting to all other numbers, and then remove all decimals in column D. Resize columns A:D so all data are visible. In cells D21, D31, and D38, apply a Top and Double Bottom Border. Select ranges **A6:G6** and **A23:G23**, and then apply the **Purple**, **Accent 4**, **Lighter 80%** color fill.

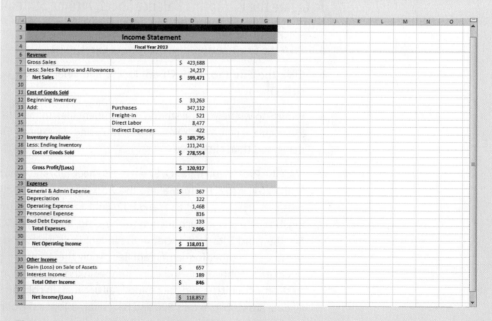

Figure 3   Income Statement worksheet

f. Click the **Cash Flow Statement worksheet tab**. Reference the appropriate cells on the Income Statement worksheet to insert values into cells C8 and C10. Calculate the increase in inventory by subtracting beginning inventory from ending inventory located on the Income Statement worksheet. Use a formula or function to calculate the totals in cells C16 and C21, apply bold and Accounting formats to the cells, and then apply conditional formatting so negative numbers will display as red text. Bold and underline the text in A7, A17, and A19; bold the text in cells A9, A13, and A21; and then increase the indent in all cells in column A that are not bold text. Apply the Accounting format to the number in cell C8, apply Comma formatting to all numbers that have no formatting, and then remove all decimals in column C. Resize columns A:C so all data are visible. In cells C16 and C21, apply a Top and Double Bottom Border. Select ranges **A7:G7**, **A17:G17**, and **A19:G19** and then apply the **Purple, Accent 4, Lighter 80%** color fill.

	A	B	C	D	E	F	G	H	I	J	K	L
1			My Sparkles									
			Jewelry for Men and Women									
2												
3			Cash Flow Statement									
4			Fiscal Year 2013									
6												
7	Cash Flow From Operations		2013	2014								
8	Net Income		$ 118,857									
9	Additions (Sources of cash)											
10	Depreciation		122									
11	Increase in Accounts Payable		14,225									
12	Increase in Accrued Income Taxes		3,248									
13	Subtractions (Uses of cash)											
14	Increase in Accounts Receivable		3,821									
15	Increase in Inventory		77,978									
16	Net Cash Flow From Operations		$ 54,653									
17	Cash Flows From Investing Activities											
18	Equipment		7,201									
19	Cash Flows Associated with Financing											
20	Activities Notes Payable		-									
21	Net Change in Cash		$ 47,452									
22												
23												

Figure 4 Cash Flow Statement worksheet

g. Click the **Product Pricing worksheet tab**. Bold the text in range A6:G6, bold and underline the text in each section heading, and then apply the **Purple, Accent 4, Lighter 80%** color fill to each section heading row. Bold the font in the category totals and grand total rows. Increase the indent of all SKUs. Calculate the retail price by multiplying the cost by the percent over cost. Use a formula or function to calculate the totals in columns F and G. Apply Accounting format to the numbers in the first cell in each section heading, category totals, and grand total cells; apply Comma formatting to all numbers without formatting; and then remove all decimals in cell range E:G. Apply conditional formatting so retail prices of $50 or more and projected totals for each product over $10,000 will display as green fill with black text, and then apply conditional formatting so projected totals for each product under $1,000 will display as light red fill with black text. Resize all columns so all data are visible. In range D91:G91, apply a Top and Double Bottom Border.

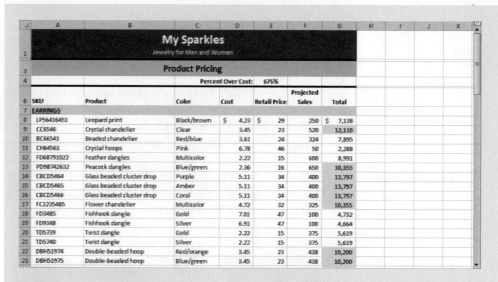

Figure 5 Product Pricing worksheet

h. Click the **Cash Flow Statement tab**. In cell D8, insert the net income by referencing the grand total on the Product Pricing worksheet. To create a worksheet that can be used for what-if analysis, add the following data and an appropriate column heading in column D, and then use a formula or function to calculate the missing values in column D. Apply the same formatting in column D that was used in column C.

Category	Amount
Depreciation	250%
Increase in Accounts Payable	300%
Increase in Accrued Income Taxes	1000%
Increase in Accounts Receivable	125%
Equipment	500%

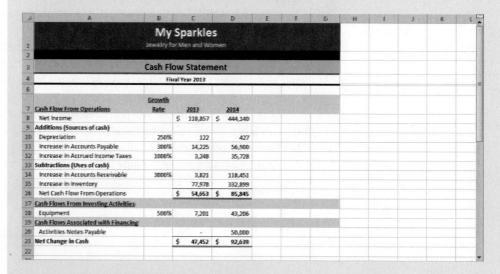

Figure 6 Revised Cash Flow Statement worksheet

i. Save your changes and then close **Lastname_Firstname_ac01_ws02_Financials**.

Creating a Database

The most important functionality of a database is to create useful information. Queries enable the user to retrieve data, filter data, calculate data totals, update data, append data, and delete records in bulk. Becoming proficient at building queries will improve your ability to manage and understand your data. Building queries helps turn data into useful information and is critical in creating quality information. Knowing the features of query design allows you to perform advanced analyses quickly.

Once you have quality information and make a decision based on that information, you now have knowledge about your organization. This knowledge can help you make decisions about your business. This **knowledge** is defined as applied information once you make the decision. For example, Laura wants to implement a customer loyalty program. If she stores customer data in the database, she could create a query that shows all customers who have referred more than five new customers over the past six months. Many functions and operators can be combined to further customize the dataset results.

> **CONSIDER THIS** | **What Would You Recommend?**
>
> What if My Sparkles wants to offer a free item from inventory, such as a buy one get one free promotion? Or offer a specific discount like $10 off a $50 purchase? What would you recommend doing in this instance? Would you need to store this in the database? How would you track this type of data?

As you work on the Excel workbook, you realize that the method in which Laura is managing her product listing is probably not the most efficient way to do so. For this problem, the goal is to determine how the products in the inventory can be best stored in an Access database. This will allow her to easily assign a SKU to each product—as of now, there is no way to ensure that a SKU is unique. Additionally, she needs an easy way to enter new products through forms and create reports that will help her manage her business. In this section, you will create an Access database. The database will require multiple tables to ensure that the database is normalized and all tables are related. Laura has been storing product data in an Excel spreadsheet; you will need to build a database from scratch and import or enter the data into the appropriate tables. Furthermore, you will generate forms and reports that will help Laura manage her inventory more easily.

> **CONSIDER THIS** | **What Purpose Would the Database Serve?**
>
> Although Excel is an excellent tool for data manipulation, it does not provide all the flexibility that a relational database can provide. What will Laura be able to do within the database that she would not be able to do in Excel? For example, does the total for each product need to be stored in a table or can it be calculated in a query?

Building the My Sparkles Database

You first need to build the tables that are needed in the database by evaluating the values on the cash flow statement. You will need to determine primary keys, foreign keys, field names, data types, field properties, and relationships. Once the tables have been created, you will create a customized data entry from along with queries and reports that display inventory totals and subtotals.

To Create the My Sparkles Database

a. Click the **Start** button, and then select **Access 2010**. Click **Blank database**. Browse to where you are storing your data files, and name your database Lastname_Firstname_ ac01_ws02_MySparkles, replacing Lastname_Firstname with your own name. Click the **Create** button to create the database.

b. Design a table to store product categories. Create appropriate fields that will describe the inventory categories and the gender for which they relate, and then assign a field to be the primary key. For all fields, enter appropriate data type descriptions, field sizes, and other field properties as needed. Save your table as tblCategory. Enter the following inventory categories into the table, and then add two new categories along with the appropriate gender. Be sure to resize fields as needed so all data are visible. Close tblCategory.

Category Name	Gender
Earrings	Women
Bracelet	Both
Necklace	Both
Ring	Both

c. Design a table to store products. Choose appropriate fields that would describe the inventory categories, and then assign a field to be the primary key. For all fields, enter appropriate data type descriptions, field sizes, captions, and other field properties as needed. Save your table as tblProduct. Enter the products into the table by importing the data from the Product Pricing worksheet, and then add two new products for one of the new categories that you added. Be sure to resize fields as needed so all data are visible. Close tblProduct.

d. Design a table to store yearly forecasted quantities. Choose appropriate fields that would describe the forecasted inventory quantities, and then assign a field to be the primary key. For all fields, enter appropriate data type descriptions, field sizes, and other field properties as needed. Include one data validation rule. Save your table as tblForecast. Design the table so Laura can use it from year to year without deleting any existing data. Enter the data into the table by importing the data from the Product Pricing worksheet, and then be sure to resize fields as needed so all data are visible. Close tblForecast.

e. Create relationships between the tables as appropriate and enforce referential integrity.

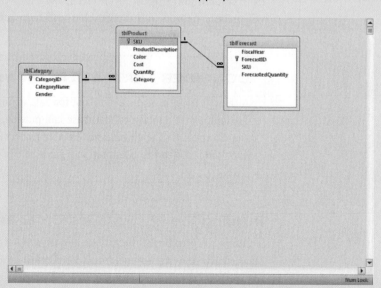

Figure 7 Relationships between the My Sparkles database tables

f. Create a query that displays the category name, SKU, product description, color, cost, gender, and forecasted quantity. Create an expression that calculates the retail price, which is 675% over cost, and then create an expression that calculates the total forecasted revenue that each product will generate in 2013. Aggregate the cost, retail price, and total forecasted revenue fields in datasheet view so that grand totals are displayed. Format all fields according to the data type. Save your query as qryForecastedTotals_initialLastname, replacing initialLastname with your own name, and then close qryForecastedTotals_initialLastname.

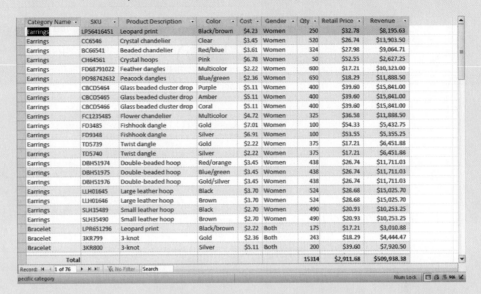

Figure 8 Results of qryForecastedTotals query

g. Create an aggregated subquery that displays the category name, gender, and forecasted revenue. Group by the category and total the forecasted revenue fields in datasheet view so that grand totals are displayed. Rename and format fields as necessary. Save your query as qryAggregatedTotals_initialLastname and then close qryAggregatedTotals_initialLastname.

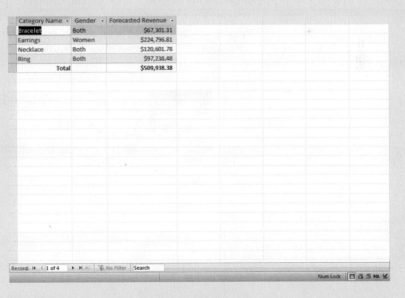

Figure 9 Results of qryAggregatedTotals query

h. Create a report from the qryForecastedTotals_initialLastname query. Add all the fields to your report and group your data by the category name. Browse to where you are storing your data files and include the **ac01_ws02_Logo** in the upper-left corner of the report.

Ensure that the heading, field names, and colors are appropriate, and then include sub-headings, totals, and a grand total for retail price and total forecasted revenue. Apply conditional formatting so retail prices over $50 and forecasted totals for each product over $10,000 will display as green fill with black text. Be sure to resize fields as needed so all data are visible, and then rename and format fields as necessary. Save your report as rptForecastedTotals_initialLastname, and then close rptForecastedTotals_initialLastname.

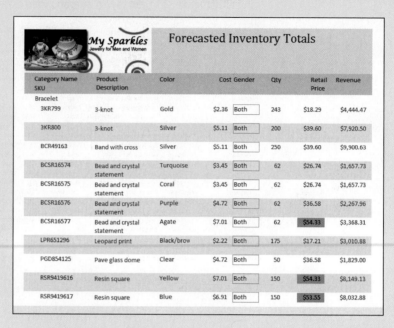

Figure 10   Results of rptForecastedTotals report

i. Create a report from the qryAggregatedTotals_initialLastname query. Add all the fields to your report. Browse to where you are storing your data files and include the **ac01_ws02_Logo** in the upper-left corner of the report. Ensure that the heading, field names, and colors are appropriate; display a grand total; and then group subtotals as a percent of the total. Be sure to resize fields as needed so all data are visible, and then rename and format fields as necessary. Save your query as rptAggregatedTotals_initialLastname, and then close rptAggregatedTotals_initialLastname.

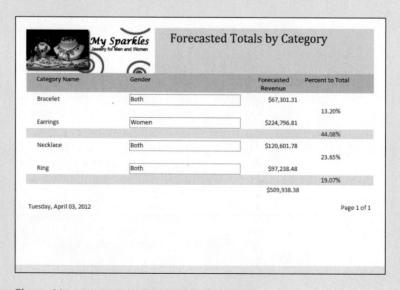

Figure 11   Results of rptForecastedTotals report

j. Create a form from the tblProduct table. Add all the fields to your form. Browse to where you are storing your data files and include the **ac01_ws02_Logo** in the upper-left corner of the form. Add a field that calculates the retail price of each product. Ensure that the heading, field names, and colors are appropriate; resize fields as needed so all data are visible; and then rename and format fields as necessary. Include five control buttons on your form so it is easier to work with the data. Save your form as frmProduct_initialLastname, and then close frmProduct_initialLastname. Create a macro that opens the form in edit mode when the database opens, and then save the macro as AutoExec.

Figure 12 Finalized frmProduct form

k. Create a PivotChart form from the qryAggregatedTotals_initialLastname query. Include the categories and forecasted revenue on your chart. Change the chart type to a 3D exploded pie chart, include data labels, and then add a legend. Ensure that the axis headings and colors are appropriate. Save your PivotChart as frmPivotChart_initialLastname, and then close frmPivotChart_initialLastname.

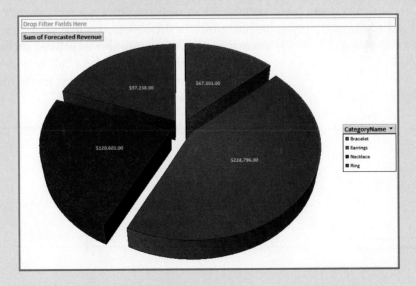

Figure 13 Finalized frmPivotChart report

All relational databases have specific words and symbols that cannot be used as field names because they have a specific meaning in Access. If you use a reserved word or symbol as a field name, Access will warn you that it is reserved and you will experience errors when working with the database. The error message you receive will not necessarily communicate that the cause of the problem stems from using a reserved word or symbol. Thus, it can be challenging to identify what needs to be revised.

Because there are hundreds if not thousands of reserved words, it is impractical to list them all. Therefore, it is important to read all warning messages thoroughly when working in Access. Remember that you can use whatever word or symbol you would like as a caption. When naming fields, create names that are compliant—Access will let you know if they are not—and then caption the fields as you so choose.

Working with Customer Data

Laura has been storing some customer data in an Excel spreadsheet. As you have been working on the database, you realize that you can help her manage her customers and their purchases more efficiently if you incorporate this data into the My Sparkles database. Although she knows the total revenue her business has generated, as noted on the income statement, she has only tracked the purchases of regular customers in her workbook.

You first need to build the tables that are needed in the database by evaluating the data in the Excel workbook. You will need to determine primary keys, foreign keys, field names, data types, field properties, and relationships. Once the tables have been created, you will create a customized data entry form along with queries and reports that display customers' purchasing history.

CONSIDER THIS | Customer Data Are Important

Customer data give companies a way to contact their customers for marketing and customer service purposes. Some customers may not want to give personal information. Do not restrict the database too much to allow for customers' personal preferences. For example, a customer may have an unlisted phone number. Consider this when determining whether data entry into a field is required because this data will be used to help Laura determine her target market for the final business plan. What other fields should be considered?

To Add Customer Data

a. Design a table to store customer data. Create appropriate fields that will describe the customers, and then assign a field to be the primary key. For all fields, enter appropriate data type descriptions, field sizes, and other field properties as needed. Save your table as tblCustomer. Import data from the Customers worksheet into the tblCustomer table from the **ac01_ws02_Customers** workbook. Be sure to resize fields as needed so all data are visible. Close tblCustomer.

b. Design a table to store purchase data. Create appropriate fields that will describe the customer purchases, and then assign a field to be the primary key. For all fields, enter appropriate data type descriptions, field sizes, and other field properties as needed. Save your table as tblPurchase. Import data from the Purchases worksheet into the tblPurchase table from the **ac01_ws02_Customers** workbook. Be sure to resize fields as needed so all data are visible. Close tblPurchase.

c. Open the Relationships window, and then relate tblCustomer and tblPurchase to the other tables in the database. Save your changes and then close the Relationships window.

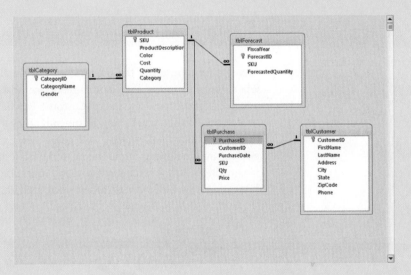

Figure 14   Updated relationships between tables

d. Create a query that displays the customer's full name in one field, purchase date, SKU, category, product description, color, quantity, and price; and then sort in ascending order by last name and then first name. Save your query as qryCustomerPurchases_initialLastname, and then close qryCustomerPurchases_initialLastname.

e. Create a report from the qryCustomerPurchases_initialLastname query. View the data by customer, and then group the data by the purchase date. Include group and grand totals. Browse to where you are storing your data files and include the **ac01_ws02_Logo** in the upper-left corner of the report. Add a field that calculates the retail price of each product. Ensure that the heading, field names, and colors are appropriate; resize fields as needed so all data are visible; and then rename and format fields as necessary. Save your report as rptCustomerPurchases_initialLastname, and then close rptCustomer-Purchases_initialLastname.

Figure 15   Finalized rptCustomerPurchases report

f. Create a form from the tblCustomer table. Add all the fields to your form. Browse to where you are storing your data files and include the **ac01_ws02_Logo** in the upper-left corner of the form. Use the qryCustomerPurchases_initialLastname query and add a subform that allows you to view all the purchases that the customers have made. Ensure that the heading, field names, and colors are appropriate; resize fields as needed so all data are visible; and then rename and format fields as necessary. Save your form as frmPurchaseHistory_initialLastname and your subform as frmPurchaseHistorySubform_initialLastname. Close frmPurchaseHistory_initialLastname.

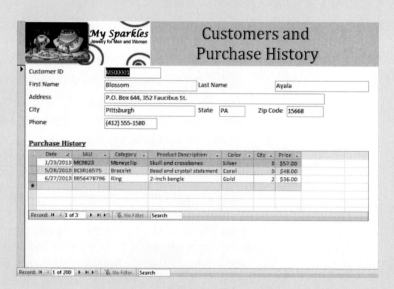

Figure 16   Finalized frmPurchaseHistory form with frmPurchaseHistorySubform

Real World Advice — Managing Customer Data

Managers determine who should have the ability to create, modify, examine, or share customer information. Nowadays businesses use options in the cloud. Regardless of the methodology that is chosen, the method should provide a cost-effective, user-friendly solution for marketing, research, sales, human resources, payroll, and information technology departments.

Requesting Additional Customer Data

The tblCustomer table contains data about Laura's regular customers and has been storing basic information; however, she has not maintained data that may be useful for determining the store's target market. A **target market** is a group of people that the business has decided to focus its marketing efforts and eventually its merchandise toward. If Laura can determine her target market and collect the right kind of data from her existing customers, she will be able to create and maintain a product mix that specifically fits the needs and preferences of that market. For example, there are many markets within the jewelry market in which companies can compete, such as independently owned retail jewelry stores; department and discount stores who have jewelry departments; online retail jewelers; and large, retail chain type jewelers—just to name a few.

Because Laura hand-crafts all her jewelry, she is considered to be a jewelry artisan and participates in the jewelry designer retail market. Although she is not well-known on a national level like some artisans, she commands high prices for her jewelry because of her regional reputation.

Real World Advice — The Devil Is in the Detail

In small retail stores, jewelers and appraisers may be involved in all facets of the work. Those who own or manage stores or shops also hire and train employees; order, market, and sell merchandise; and perform other managerial duties. Designers need a high degree of skill and must pay attention to detail.

Before Laura can determine who her target market is, she needs to collect some more information from her customers to learn more about her market segmentation. **Market segmentation** is a result of learning that all prospective customers are not alike, and that the same general appeal will not interest all prospects. Thus, it becomes crucial to develop different marketing strategies based on the differences among prospects in order to effectively market to all prospective customers for a specific product.

Real World Advice — You Cannot Market to Everyone

Some managers believe that everyone will want to purchase the product they manufacture or sell. This is a misconception. Managers must determine who is most likely to purchase their product or service and go after that market segment. Once these specific customers have been defined, the business can establish a marketing mix strategy that will satisfy the target market.

Laura has decided that she will send a postcard that includes a survey and coupon to her regular customers. The postcard will ask customers to give more information about them, and in return, customers will receive 20 percent off any purchase. In this section, you will finalize the postcard and then create a mail merge with the tblCustomer table in the My Sparkles database.

Real World Advice · Real Organizations Use Target Marketing

Organizations like Kraft and CVS Caremark use target marketing to ensure that their product is reaching as many prospective customers as possible. Kraft manufactured a different version of the Oreo to target consumers in China. Kraft executives live and work in China so they can learn what Chinese consumers would prefer in order to maximize their profits. CVS Caremark's target market is women, because they make up 80 percent of the pharmacy chain's customers. CVS has marketed its stores to help women who are continuously multitasking and recently redesigned nearly 20 percent of its stores to fit women's needs, including shorter wait times for prescriptions, wider and better-lit shopping aisles, and more beauty products.

To Finalize the Postcard and Create a Mail Merge

a. Click the **Start** button, and then select **Word 2010**.

b. Click the **File tab**, click **Open**, locate and select **ac01_ws02_Postcard**, and then click **Open**.

c. Browse to where you are storing your student files. In the File name box, type Lastname_ Firstname_ac01_ws02_Postcard, replacing Lastname_Firstname with your actual name, and then click **Save**.

d. Using the figure below as a guideline, modify the postcard by adding text boxes to add the coupon, store hours, and return address, and then add the My Sparkles logo. Save your changes.

Figure 17   Front of the postcard

Figure 18 Back of the postcard

e. Create a mail merge and use the tblCustomer table in the My Sparkles database as your recipient list. Insert the appropriate merged fields on the front of the postcard. Click **Finish & Merge** and merge the document so you can edit individual documents if necessary. Save the document as Lastname_Firstname_ac01_ws02_PostcardMerged. Close Lastname_Firstname_ac01_ws02_PostcardMerged.

Figure 19 First postcard after mail merge performed

Developing a Target Market

Now that Laura is beginning to receive postcards back from her regular customers, she is going to be able to learn more about her demographic segmentation. **Demographic segmentation** is the most popular method for separating groups, primarily because consumer needs typically match demographic categories, but also because demographic variables are relatively easy to acquire and measure. Forms of demographic segmentation include, but are not limited to, age, education, income, and marital status.

By Laura knowing who her typical customer is, she will be able to determine her marketing mix—a method used in marketing products. The **marketing mix**, coined in 1953 by Neil Borden, is vital when determining a product or brand's unique selling point and is frequently synonymous with the four P's—price, product, promotion, and place. These elements are considered when planning a marketing strategy, and any of the elements may be enhanced, removed, or modified in order to create the strategy necessary to efficiently and effectively sell a product.

Quick Reference / What Are the Four P's?

When planning a marketing strategy, any of the four P's elements may be enhanced, removed, or modified in order to create the strategy necessary to efficiently and effectively sell a product.

Element	Description
Price	The price is the amount a customer pays for the product and is very important as it determines the company's profit and thus its survival. Modifying the price can have a major impact on the marketing strategy because it can affect both the demand and sales. Managers should establish a price that complements the other elements of the marketing mix.
Product	A product is a tangible or intangible item that fulfills a consumer's needs or wants. A tangible item is one that can be felt physically such as a necklace, shirt, car, or apple. An intangible item is a service-based item such as a car rental, plane ticket, or hotel room.
Promotion	Promotion includes elements such as advertising, public relations, personal selling, and sales promotion.
Place	Place is synonymous with distribution and refers to placing a product in a location that is convenient for consumers to purchase.

Figure 20   Explanation of the four P's

In 1993, Robert Lauterborn proposed a four C's classification, which serves as a postscript to the four P's as it is more consumer oriented and attempts to better fit the movement from mass marketing to niche marketing. **Mass marketing** is when an organization decides to overlook market segment differences and aim for selling to the whole market by focusing on high sales and low prices. Traditionally, mass marketing has focused on radio, television, and newspapers as the technique used to reach a wide-ranging audience. By reaching the largest audience possible, exposure to the product is maximized. In theory, this large exposure would directly correlate with higher sales. A business that focuses on **niche marketing** is addressing a need for a product or service that is not being addressed by conventional suppliers. A **niche market** has a narrowly defined group of potential customers such as Rolls Royce and Bentley Motors.

Quick Reference — What Are the Four C's?

Many people who have taken a course in marketing have learned about the four P's. Bob Lauterborn, professor of advertising at the University of North Carolina, followed the success of new products introduced into the United States and found that 80 percent of new products fail each year. Whether you decide to utilize the four P's or four C's methodology, you must learn about your market and know who your customers are.

Element	Description
Cost	Cost reflects the total cost of ownership and is affected by many factors. Examples include the customer's cost to change to or implement the new product or service and the customer's cost for not choosing a competitor's product or service.
Consumer	The focus of consumer shifts to satisfying consumer needs. Organizations that follow this model believe in making products that satisfy their customers and are generally prepared to offer customizable products. This element is only applicable for smaller market segments and not mass markets.
Communication	Communication embodies a broader focus than promotions. It can include advertising, public relations, personal selling, viral marketing, and any form of communication between the organization and the consumer.
Convenience	Convenience is similar to placement in the traditional marketing mix. With Internet sales on the rise and hybrid models of purchasing, place is becoming less relevant.

Figure 21 Explanation of the four C's

Identifying the Target Market

According to Phillip Kotler and Gary Armstrong in *Principles of Marketing*, there are three phases involved in developing a target market—market segmentation, market targeting, and market positioning. An organization needs to determine its value proposition and must be relevant to its target market, and because of this, the target market must be clearly defined.

It is not uncommon for an organization to have to refocus and reexamine its targeting, especially if it was not clearly identified beforehand. The goal is to describe the target market in a way in which consumers realize you are communicating a message directly to them. This often requires companies to center on their target market. In order to identify a target market and market segmentations, you need to evaluate demographic data.

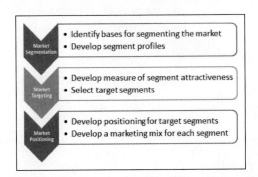

Figure 22 Steps in developing a target market

Updating the Database for Additional Customer Data

Laura is beginning to receive postcards back from her regular customers. She has been entering this new data into an Excel spreadsheet because there is nowhere in the database to enter the data. In this section, you will modify the database to allow for the additional demographic data, enter the new data, and create a query and report that help Laura learn about her customers.

To Modify the Database for Additional Customer Data

a. Design a table to store demographic data. Use Customer ID as the primary key, format the field as a lookup field that looks up the customer's first and last name in the tblCustomer table, and then sort the field in ascending order by last and first name. Enable data integrity and then set the field so it does not delete any records from the related table. Create appropriate fields that will describe the customers' demographic data. For all fields, enter appropriate data type descriptions, field sizes, and other field properties as needed. Save your table as **tblDemographics**. Import data from the Demographics worksheet in the **ac01_ws02_Customers** workbook into the tblDemographics table. Aggregate the cost, retail price, and total forecasted revenue fields in Datasheet view so that grand totals are displayed. Be sure to resize fields as needed so all data are visible. Close tblDemographics.

Education	CustomerID	Age	Salary Range	Marital Status	Employment Status	Click to Add
High School	Ayala	46-55	Below $35K	Divorced	Part-time	
Some College	Brooks	Over 55	$36-45K	Single	Not Employed	
Post-Graduate Degree	Lewis	36-45	$55-65K	Widowed	Not Employed	
Post-Graduate Degree	Santana	36-45	$45-55K	Married	Not Employed	
Post-Graduate Degree	Clay	Below 25	$45-55K	Single	Retired	
High School	Ellis	Over 55	Over $65K	Single	Not Employed	
Post-Graduate Degree	Charles	Below 25	$55-65K	Divorced	Not Employed	
High School	Mclaughlin	Over 55	$55-65K	Divorced	Retired	
Some College	Downs	Below 25	$36-45K	Significant Other	Full-time	
Some College	Nichols	46-55	Below $35K	Single	Not Employed	
Some College	Mendoza	26-35	Below $35K	Significant Other	Part-time	
High School	Melendez	Over 55	Over $65K	Single	Student	
Post-Graduate Degree	Pickett	Over 55	Below $35K	Married	Retired	
Graduate Degree	Stein	36-45	$45-55K	Significant Other	Part-time	
Some College	Sandoval	26-35	Below $35K	Married	Part-time	
Undergraduate Degree	Garza	46-55	$36-45K	Widowed	Student	
Undergraduate Degree	Sharpe	46-55	$45-55K	Single	Part-time	
Graduate Degree	Moreno	36-45	$45-55K	Significant Other	Retired	
Post-Graduate Degree	Tanner	Below 25	Over $65K	Single	Student	
Some College	Meadows	Over 55	$45-55K	Married	Student	
Graduate Degree	Roach	Below 25	$45-55K	Divorced	Not Employed	
Some College	Phillips	Below 25	$45-55K	Significant Other	Retired	
High School	Bartlett	Below 25	Over $65K	Divorced	Part-time	
High School	Boone	36-45	Over $65K	Single	Full-time	
High School	Miles	26-35	$36-45K	Significant Other	Not Employed	

Record: 1 of 53   No Filter   Search

Figure 23   tblDemographics table after data import

b. Create a crosstab query from the tblDemographics table. Use age and marital status as the row headings, salary range as the column heading, and then count the customer IDs. Save your query as qryDemographicsSalary_initialLastname. Close qryDemographicsSalary_initialLastname.

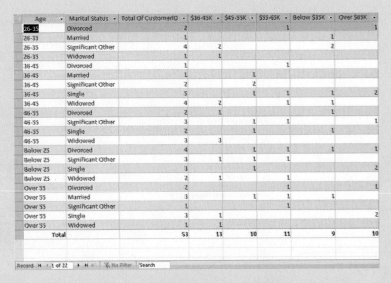

Figure 24   Crosstab query of customer demographics

c. Create a report from the qryDemographicsSalary_initialLastname query. Group the data by age and marital status. Click the **Summary Options** button. Only display the summary for each salary category, and then calculate the percent of the total for sums. Save your report as rptDemographicsSalary_initialLastname. Change the report title to Demographics Report by Salary, and then resize fields as necessary. Remove the Summary labels, and then format the report to make it visually appealing. Save your changes, close rptDemographicsSalary_initialLastname, and then close Access.

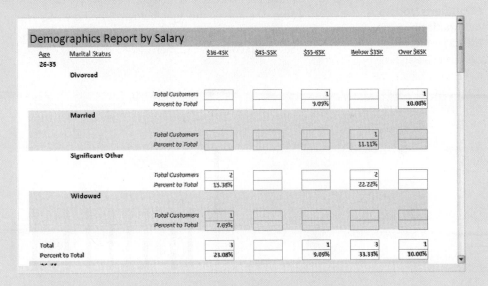

Figure 25   Demographics Report by Salary

d. Open the **Lastname_Firstname_ac01_ws02_Financials** workbook, insert a new blank worksheet in front of the Pro-forma Balance Sheet worksheet, and then name the worksheet Demographic Analysis. Import the tblDemographics table as a PivotTable Report into the Demographic Analysis worksheet. Add age as the column label; add education, salary range, and marital status as the row labels; and then add employment status as the value. Click cell **A1**, type Demographics Report, and then resize columns as necessary. Change the PivotTable style to **Pivot Style Light 19**. Insert a slicer for salary range and marital status, and then change the slicer style to **Slicer Style Light 4**. Resize the slicers as needed, move both to the right of the PivotTable report, and then align vertically. Using the slicers, filter the data to display a salary range of $55,000 to $65,000 and divorced as the marital status.

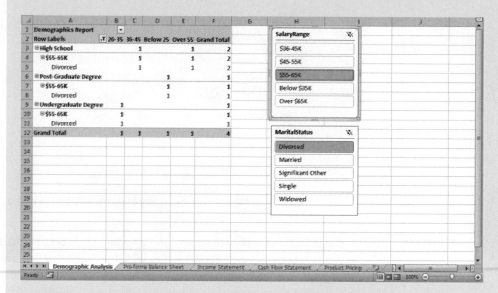

Figure 26   PivotTable report filtered by salary range and marital status

SIDE NOTE

A Picture's Worth 1,000 Words

A picture is worth 1,000 words and it is easier to create a chart in Excel than in Access. Many professionals export data from a database to Excel for further analysis.

SIDE NOTE

PivotCharts Update Automatically

As Laura gathers more customer data and enters it into the database, the PivotChart will update automatically and create a more varied output.

e. Clear the marital status on the PivotTable. Click cell **A14**, insert a PivotChart, and then move the chart to a new worksheet. Name the worksheet Demographic PivotChart. Filter the age so the ages below 25 and over 55 are not included, and the filter the salary so the salaries below $35,000 and between $45,000 and $55,000 are displayed. Save your changes and then Close Excel.

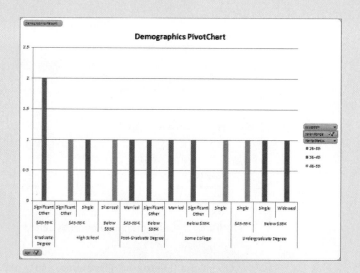

Figure 27   PivotChart filtered by salary range and age

Creating a Persona

Now that Laura has analyzed the demographics and determined her market segmentations, she will be able to create her persona. A **persona** is a fictional character that is generated to represent the customers within a targeted demographic and is primarily developed to help determine where there are opportunities and areas for improvement. Personas are often used together with market segmentation. Bonnie Rind in *The Power of the Persona* explains that while a persona is not a real person, he or she must feel like a real person to everyone in the company. Thus, in addition to facts related to his or her use of the product, you should have the following basic knowledge about the persona:

- Name, age, and education
- Socioeconomic class and socioeconomic desires
- Life or career goals, fears, hopes, and attitudes
- Reasons for using the product
- Needs and expectations of the product
- Intellectual and physical skills that can be applied to the product
- Personal biases about the product

Many organizations do not include images of their personas when developing them; however, it does help employees understand who their customers could be.

Both market segmentation and personas provide useful information—one informs the other. After analyzing the data within the database and from postcards that have been redeemed since you added the tblDemographics table, Laura has learned a great deal about her customers.

Demographic Segmentation	Results of Male Customers	Results of Female Customers
Age	Customers within this segment tend to be between the ages of 36–45.	Customers within this segment tend to be between the ages of 26–35.
Salary Range	Customers within this segment tend to have salaries that are over $65,000.	Customers within this segment tend to have salaries that fall within the range of $36,000 to $45,000.
Marital Status	Customers within this segment tend to be married or have a significant other.	Customers within this segment tend to be married or have a significant other.
Employment Status	Customers within this segment have a full-time job.	Customers within this segment have a full-time job.
Education	Customers within this segment have furthered their education after high school.	Customers within this segment have furthered their education after high school.

Figure 28   Results of the customer demographics analysis

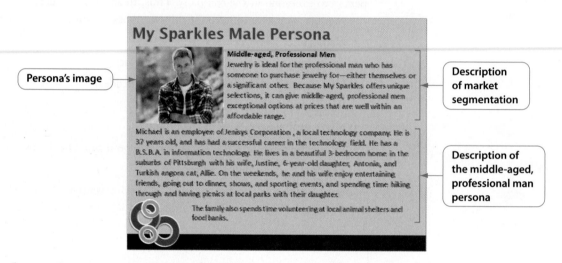

Figure 29   Male persona for the typical My Sparkles customer

Because the persona encompasses specific characteristics within a market segment, Laura would like you to help develop a portrait of someone who is ready to purchase her products. She has already had time to create the male persona of the typical My Sparkles customer. In this section, you will create a female persona of the typical My Sparkles customer.

To Create the Female Persona

a. Click the **Start** button, and then select **PowerPoint 2010**.

b. Click the **File tab**, click **Open**, locate and select **ac01_ws02_Persona**, and then click **Open**.

c. Browse to where you are storing your student files. In the File name box, type Lastname_ Firstname_ac01_ws02_Persona, replacing Lastname_Firstname with your actual name and then click **Save**.

d. Browse to where you are storing your data files and then insert the **ac01_ws02_FemalePersona** image in place of the Replace with Photo text box. Based on the image and the results of the customer demographics analysis, create the overview of the persona and the female persona details in the appropriate text boxes. Check your spelling and grammar, save your changes, and then close Lastname_Firstname_ac01_ws02_Persona.

Real World Advice | Developing a Persona Is Always a Work in Progress

Describing and refining your organization's persona is always a work in progress. As a manager, you should always be soliciting customer feedback. One of the best ways to learn about your customers is to contact them right after they have made a purchase. If they purchased an item from your website, it is best practice to offer a small discount on their next purchase if they complete a survey. The objective is to find methods of obtaining information from your customers in a manner that is comfortable to them.

Analyzing the Company and Industry

Now that Laura knows more about her customers, the evaluation of her market has not ended. When applying for a loan or seeking out an investor, at a minimum they would want to see an analysis of your company as well as the industry in which your organization conducts business or will conduct business. Many models are available that aid in this type of analysis, but the two commonly used models in the business world are a SWOT analysis and Porter's Five Forces model.

Developing a SWOT Analysis

A **SWOT analysis**, developed by Albert Humphrey in the 1960s, is a strategic planning technique used to evaluate the Strengths, Weaknesses, Opportunities, and Threats of a project or business venture. This analysis helps an organization accomplish its objectives and determine the obstacles that must be overcome or minimized in order to achieve its desired results. To achieve this, organizations perform an environmental analysis and separate the information obtained into internal issues—strengths and weaknesses—and external issues—opportunities and threats.

Additionally, a SWOT analysis can be used for matching and converting. Matching is used to find competitive advantages by matching the strengths that were determined in the analysis to potential opportunities. Converting is the process of converting weaknesses or threats into strengths or opportunities. Not all weaknesses or threats can be converted. Thus, if the threats or weaknesses cannot be converted into strengths or opportunities, a company should try to minimize or avoid them.

Managers will often collect data to perform analyses and, because of this, find it necessary to invest money in the research process. By doing so, marketing managers are able to perform an accurate marketing analysis. Marketing managers practice a variety of techniques to conduct market research, but some of the more common practices include:

- Qualitative marketing research, such as focus groups
- Quantitative marketing research, such as statistical surveys
- Experimental techniques, such as pilot tests
- Observational techniques, such as on-site observations

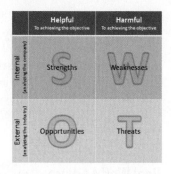

Figure 30   SWOT analysis with the four elements

For example, Starbucks has been in business since 1971 and began as a roaster and retailer of whole bean and ground coffee, tea, and spices with a single store in Seattle's Pike Place Market. Today, the company has more than 17,000 retail stores in over 55 countries. This company has done many things the right way. However, this does not mean that there are no other opportunities to explore, nor does it mean that Starbucks does not face weaknesses or threats. A great company continually evaluates its own company along with its position in the marketplace.

SWOT Objective	Company or Industry	Description
Strengths	Analyze the company	Strengths are the characteristics of the business that give it an advantage over others. Examples of strengths include reputation of, or expertise within, the organization.
Weaknesses	Analyze the company	Weaknesses, also known as limitations, are characteristics that place the team at a disadvantage relative to others. Examples of weaknesses include lack of funding or minimal technological knowledge.
Opportunities	Analyze the industry	Opportunities are elements in the environment that can help improve performance. Examples of opportunities include corporate mergers—this could help gain market share—or the development of new products.
Threats	Analyze the industry	Elements in the environment that could cause trouble for the business. Threats could include an economic downfall or new competition.

Figure 31   Setting the SWOT analysis objectives

With a little practice, a SWOT analysis can be created by anyone. If you were to create a SWOT analysis for Starbucks, it may resemble the following analysis. Certainly more information could be included beneath Strengths, Weaknesses, Opportunities, and Threats.

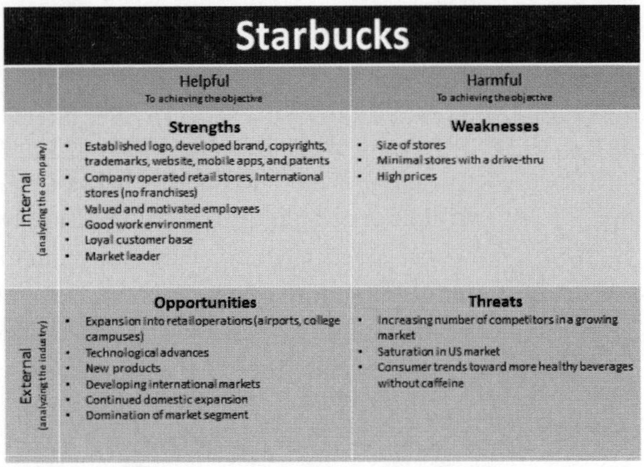

Figure 32 SWOT analysis for Starbucks

Real World Advice **A SWOT Analysis Is a Guide for Managers**

When constructing a SWOT analysis for your business plan, you should be realistic about the strengths and weaknesses of your organization. Differentiate between where your organization is today, and where it could be in the future. Additionally, remember to be specific and create your analysis while relating to the competition. Finally, keep your SWOT analysis short and simple, and elude complexity and over-analysis because much of the information included on your analysis will be subjective. Best practice is to use the analysis as a guide.

Because the SWOT analysis is a useful way to analyze a company and industry, Laura would like you to help create this analysis. She has already created a template for you to use. In this section, you will create a SWOT analysis for My Sparkles and the jewelry retailer industry.

To Create a SWOT Analysis

a. In PowerPoint, click the **File tab**, click **Open**, locate and select **ac01_ws02_Analysis**, and then click **Open**.

b. Browse to where you are storing your student files. In the File name box, type Lastname_ Firstname_ac01_ws02_Analysis, replacing Lastname_Firstname with your actual name, and then click **Save**.

c. Click **Slide 1**, if necessary. Based on what you have learned about Laura's business, determine a minimum of two Strengths, Weaknesses, Opportunities, and Threats. Check your spelling and grammar, and then save your changes.

SIDE NOTE
Learn More
To learn more about the jewelry industry, visit **www. nationaljeweler.com/nj/ fashion**.

Analyzing an Industry Using Porter's Five Forces Model

In 1979, Michael Porter of Harvard Business School developed the Five Forces model to use as a framework for industry analysis and business strategy development. The **Five Forces model** is used to determine the competitive power and consequently the attractiveness of a market. In this situation, attractiveness refers to the overall profitability within a specific industry. An unattractive industry is one where the unification of these five forces acts to decrease overall profitability. A very unattractive industry is one that is approaching pure competition where obtainable profits for all organizations are driven to normal profit margins. However, this does not mean that all businesses within the industry will generate the same profitability.

Real World Advice — Many Organizations Perform Strategic Analyses

Regardless of whether organizations are for-profit, nonprofit, government agencies, or in the academic sector, they all have competition. Because of this, they all need to perform a SWOT and Five Forces analyses at some point and most will perform these analyses on a regular basis, generally every year.

Michael Porter in *Competitive strategy: Techniques for analyzing industries and competitors* explains how he analyzes an industry by looking at the barriers to entry, threat of substitutes, bargaining power of suppliers, bargaining power of buyers, and the competitive position of industry rivals. These forces can affect an organization's ability to assist its customers and return a profit. A change in any of the five forces typically requires a business to reexamine the marketplace given the change in industry information.

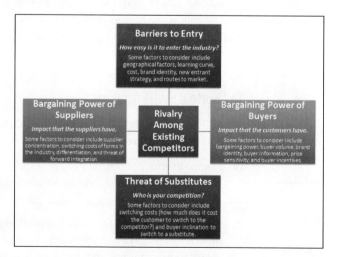

Figure 33 Porter's Five Forces that determines industry attractiveness and profitability

New entrants—meaning new companies—to an industry can increase competition, thus decreasing the market's appeal. The threat of new entrants essentially depends on the barriers to entry. High entry barriers exist in some industries, such as the computer operating system software industry. Other industries are very easy to enter, or have low barriers to entry, such as the restaurant industry. In order to determine the key barriers to entry for an industry, you need to have the following basic knowledge about this category.

Factor	Description
Economies of scale	Economies of scale give big companies access to a larger market by allowing them to operate with greater geographical reach. There are two types of economies of scale:
	External economies—the cost per unit depends on the size of the industry, not the firm.
	Internal economies—the cost per unit depends on size of the individual firm.
	Phar-Mor was a chain of discount drug stores based out of Youngstown, Ohio. Low prices were advertised to bring in a large volume of sales with the slogan "Phar-Mor power buying gives you Phar-Mor buying power." They purchased large quantities from suppliers, giving Phar-Mor better pricing and lower input costs. Ultimately the company passed those savings onto its consumers.
Capital or investment requirements	Capital or investment requirements refer to the amount of funding a company will need to enter the market. Capital investment decisions that involve the purchase of items—such as land, machinery, buildings, or equipment—are among the most important decisions undertaken by a manager. These decisions typically involve committing large sums of money, which will affect the business over a number of years.
Customer switching costs	Switching costs are the costs that a consumer experiences as a result of changing suppliers, brands, or products. Although the most common switching costs are monetary, there are also psychological, effort-based, and time-based switching costs. For example, many cellular phone carriers charge very high termination fees for canceling a contract. Cell phone carriers anticipate that the costs involved with switching to another carrier will be high enough to prevent their customers from doing so.
Access to industry distribution channels	Companies can sell through a single channel or through multiple channels such as direct sales, consultants, dealers, or retail.
Probability of retaliation from existing industry companies	Companies can and will react to a new company's entrance into the market. The question is, "How?" Giant Eagle is an aggressively growing company with 175 corporate and 54 independently owned and operated supermarkets and 168 fuel and convenience stores located in western Pennsylvania, Ohio, West Virginia, and Maryland. In 2012, the Pittsburgh area stores are dealing with a competitor—Bottom Dollar Food—entering the market. Bottom Dollar Food is known for offering name brand merchandise at below-competitor prices. Giant Eagle is considering opening some of its Valu King Food Market stores in the Pittsburgh region to compete with its new competitor. If this occurs, one store would even be right next door to Bottom Dollar Food!

Figure 34 Factors to consider when analyzing the barriers to entry

Suppliers are the companies that supply materials and other products to organizations within the industry. The price of items purchased from suppliers—such as raw materials if the company manufactures goods or inventory if it sells finished products—can have a substantial impact on an organization's profitability. If suppliers have high bargaining power over an organization, then in theory the organization's industry is less attractive. When determining the bargaining power of suppliers, consider the following factors:

- There are many buyers and few suppliers.
- There are undifferentiated, highly valued products.
- Suppliers threaten to integrate forward into the industry, such as brand manufacturers threatening to open retail outlets.
- Buyers do not threaten to integrate backward into supply.
- The industry is not a crucial customer group to the suppliers.

Buyers are the people or organizations who create demand in the industry. The bargaining power of customers is their ability to put an organization under pressure, which also affects the customer's understanding of price changes. When determining the bargaining power of buyers, consider the following factors to determine whether the bargaining power of buyers is high:

- There are few buyers and many sellers.
- Switching costs are low.
- Buyers can easily create the seller's product themselves.
- Customers can purchase large volumes of identical products from the seller.
- Substitute products are available on the market.
- The customer is price conscious and well-educated about the product.

The threat of substitutes is the availability of a product that a consumer can purchase in place of another product that offers similar benefits. According to Porter, the threat of substitutes shapes the competitive structure of an industry. Alternatively, the shortage of similar substitute products makes an industry less competitive and increases the potential profit for the organizations in the industry. For example, consider the beverage industry because of the tremendous number of competitors. Pepsi would not be a substitute for Coca-Cola; however, coffee, tea, milk, juice, and water would be. The threat of substitute products depends on the following factors:

- Buyers' willingness to substitute
- The relative price and performance of substitutes
- The costs of switching to substitutes

The fifth force, rivalry among existing competitors within an industry, refers to the competitive position of industry rivals by analyzing their strengths and weaknesses. If rivalry is aggressive, competitors are attempting to take both the profit and market share from each other, which reduces potential profit for all industry organizations. According to Porter, the intensity of rivalry among organizations is one of the main forces that form an industry's competitive structure and influence the ability of existing firms to achieve profitability. High intensity of rivalry means competitors are aggressively targeting each other's markets and aggressively pricing products. This can decrease profit potential for the existing organizations. Conversely, low intensity of rivalry makes an industry less competitive and increases potential profit for the existing organizations.

If you were to analyze the specialty coffee industry—the industry in which Starbucks conducts business—using Porter's Five Forces model, it may resemble the following analysis. Once all factors are considered, you should determine whether or not each force is high, low, or mixed—contains both high and low factors.

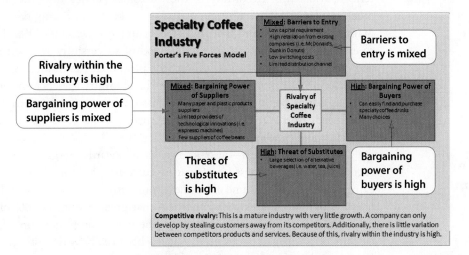

Figure 35 Porter's Five Forces analysis for the specialty coffee industry

CONSIDER THIS | **Can You Explain a Five Forces Analysis?**

Now that you have reviewed the specialty coffee industry analysis, can you explain what it means? Is it encouraging for a company in this industry to have the barriers to entry and bargaining power of suppliers categorized as mixed? Is it encouraging for a company in this industry to have the threat of substitutes, bargaining power of buyers, and rivalry within the industry categorized as high? Does this industry have anything to be concerned about? Do you think this industry is here to stay or is it a fad? Should the companies in this industry be concerned with it being considered a mature market?

Because Porter's Five Forces analysis is a beneficial way to analyze an industry, Laura would like you to help create this analysis. She has already created a template for you to use. In this section, you will create an industry analysis for the specialty jewelry retail industry.

To Create an Analysis Using the Five Forces Model

a. Click **Slide 2**, and then determine the factors for the barriers to entry, bargaining power of suppliers, bargaining power of buyers, and threat of substitutes forces. On the line in front of each force, indicate whether each force is high, low, or mixed.

b. In the text box at the bottom of the slide, discuss the competitive rivalry, and then indicate whether this force is high, low, or mixed. Check your spelling and grammar, save your changes, and then close PowerPoint.

Creating a Customer Loyalty Program

Loyalty programs are a technique used to reward your best customers and build long-term relationships. According to the Customer Service Institute, it costs five times as much to attract a new customer as it does to keep an existing one satisfied. A study by Marketing Metrics found that the typical company has a 60–70% likelihood of reselling to existing customers, 20–40% likelihood of successfully selling to former customers, and only a 5–20% chance of selling to a prospective customer. According to Frederick Reicheld in *The Loyalty Effect and Loyalty Rules*, loyalty leaders grow on average more than twice as fast as the industry average across a wide variety of industries. Because of this, Laura needs to ensure that her existing customers are satisfied and want to shop at her store time and time again.

A **loyalty program**—also known as a rewards program—is frequently used to encourage repeat business from existing customers by providing gifts and perks that are earned based on the volume of business your customers do with you. Laura has decided to offer a program—Pieces with Panache—that gives customers 50% off one item after the purchase of five regularly priced items. She needs you to develop a flyer to distribute to customers. She began to design it, but has been too busy designing, creating, and selling jewelry to complete it—a good problem to have!

To Create a Marketing Flyer for a Loyalty Program

a. Click the **Start** button, and then select **Word 2010**.

b. Click the **File tab**, click **Open**, locate and select **ac01_ws02_LoyaltyFlyer**, and then click **Open**.

c. Browse to where you are storing your student files. In the File name box, type Lastname_Firstname_ac01_ws02_LoyaltyFlyer, replacing Lastname_Firstname with your actual name, and then click **Save**.

d. Laura wrote most of what she would like to see on the flyer, but needs some input from you. Use the following to complete the text portion of the flyer. Maintain the formatting that she has already set up for you, unless you change formatting to make the flyer more appealing.

Tagline	PIECES WITH PANACHE
Subheading	You Are Our Jewel! Format the font to match the pink color in the tagline and then click **Bold**.
Overview	Earn 50% off anything in the store! Purchase 5 pieces of regularly priced jewelry and qualify for this special discount.
Rules and Conditions	• Discount is non-transferrable. • Retail price cannot exceed the average dollar amount of the 5 items purchased. • Discount may be used on regularly, priced and sale merchandise. • Create and insert two ideas of your own

e. Insert **ac01_ws02_Jewelry** in place of the Insert photo here text box, and then resize the image so that the white background is completely covered. Check your spelling and grammar, save your changes, and then close Word.

Figure 36   Marketing flyer for the loyalty program

Compiling Your Business Plan

To assemble a suitable business plan, you need to be able to think strategically, investigate and review the market, convince people to give you information, understand financial statements, develop your ideas clearly, and communicate your ideas to others. To successfully run a business, you need all these skills and more. When you write a business plan, you develop numerous skills needed to run a business. Consider the work you have completed thus far. You have developed much of the information needed to construct your business plan. In this section, you will compile your business plan and create any outstanding components needed to finalize the plan.

Develop the Components of a Business Plan

A business plan is a decision-making tool with no specific content because the content and format of the business plan is determined by the organization's goals and audience—such as a bank or investor. In this section, you will create a PowerPoint presentation that compiles all the documents you created for Laura. You have created financial documents, marketing documents, and a database for Laura's business. You now need to compile the documents needed when Laura meets with a bank's loan officer or investor. This will make it easier for her to present her ideas to potential investors because you can fit each document you created on one slide. According to Harvard Business School, in order to appropriately construct a business plan, you need to include the following components.

Component	Description
Cover page and table of contents	This makes the report look more professional and the content easy to find.
Executive summary	Short section at the beginning of the report; it is intended to provide a neutral overview—it is not an introduction. This should be the last task you perform.
Business description	Usually begins with a short description of the industry along with a discussion of the present outlook as well as future possibilities. Also provide information on all the various markets within the industry, including any new products or developments that will positively or unfavorably affect your business.
Business environment analysis	Examine the industry and determine the overall environment. You can use tools like Porter's Five Forces model.
Industry background	Organize companies into industrial groupings based on similar production processes, similar products, or similar behavior in financial markets.
Competitor analysis	Assessment of the strengths and weaknesses of current and potential competitors.
Market analysis	Reviews the attractiveness and the changing aspects of the market.
Marketing plan	Consists of a list of actions that dovetail with the marketing strategy.
Operations plan	Outlines the day-to-day functions of running a business.
Management summary	Includes all of the applicable information about personnel, anticipated growth, and how the company is organized.
Financial plan	A series of phases that are executed, or goals that are accomplished, which relate to the business's financial affairs.
References	Cite any sources you may have used to support your data.
Attachments and milestones	Includes anything that can help support your business's ability to be successful—letters from customers, community awards, certifications, and so on.

Figure 37 Components included in a business plan

Before you begin writing your business plan, take a moment to reflect on where your company is and where it is going. This is the process of planning your plan. Planning is one of the most important tasks you will perform in business. Have you ever heard the cliché, "If you fail to plan, plan to fail"? There is a great deal of truth in this statement. According to statistics published by the Small Business Administration (SBA), 7 out of 10 new companies last at least two years, and 51% last at least five years. Much of this has to do with poor planning. It is critical for all businesses to have a business plan. Many small businesses fail because of major weaknesses in their planning. It must be realistic and based on accurate, current information and refined forecasts for the future. Think about where you currently are, where you want to be in five years, and then determine your goals and objectives.

The second page of your business plan will be your executive summary. An executive summary is not an introduction, but a summary of the critical findings within the report. The first of five key elements the summary should describe is the business, its products, and the market it will serve. You should clarify what will be sold, to whom, and why the business will hold a competitive advantage in the marketplace. Secondly, describe the important financial points of the business including sales, profit, cash flow, and return on investment. **Return on investment** (ROI) is a method used to measure performance and evaluate whether an investment will pay for itself or help generate more revenue. To calculate ROI, the benefit (return) of an investment is divided by the cost of the investment—the result is expressed as a percentage or a ratio. Third, clearly explain the money or investment needed to start the business and to expand when the time arises. It should detail how the funding will be used. Fourth, state appropriate information about the company, such as its legal arrangement—for example, whether the business has been established as a corporation, when it was formed, the principal owners, and key personnel. Finally, note any accomplishments within the company that are necessary for the business to succeed.

The operations plan section is typically divided into two parts—stage of development and production process. The stage of development section should describe how the products will be made and identify the problems that may occur during production. Additionally, it should explain who the suppliers are, their prices, terms, and conditions and a description of any arrangements that have been made—or will be made—if these suppliers fail in providing you with raw materials. The production process section should outline the details of the business's day-to-day operations—general information, the physical plant, equipment, assets, materials, production, inventory, feasibility, cost, and any special requirements.

Component	Description
General information	This outlines hours of operation and the days the business will be open.
Physical plant	What is the size and type of location in which the business is currently conducting its day-to-day operations?
Equipment	Describe the equipment necessary to operate the business. Further explain how much is needed, its worth and cost, and financing arrangements, if any.
Assets	Assets include items such as land, buildings, inventory, furniture, equipment, and vehicles.
Materials	Note where the raw materials will be obtained and explain what terms have been negotiated with suppliers.
Production	Explain how long it takes to produce an item and when production will begin. Include elements that may affect the time frame of production and how potential problems will be handled, such as rush orders.
Inventory	Explain how inventory will be tracked and managed.
Feasibility	Describe any product testing, price testing, or prototype testing that has been conducted.
Cost	Estimate the costs associated with the products.
Special requirements	Any special requirements—such as water or power needs, ventilation, drainage—should be detailed along with what has been done to secure the necessary zoning permissions.

Figure 38 Components included in the day-to-day operations section of a business plan

Laura would like you to compile a business plan for her. You already have most of the data needed in order to do so. Laura will provide you with the operations plan, which you will need to input into your document.

To Create a Business Plan

a. Click the **Start** button, and then select **PowerPoint 2010**.

b. Click the **File tab**, click **Open**, locate and select **ac01_ws02_BusinessPlan**, and then click **Open**.

c. Browse to where you are storing your student files. In the File name box, type Lastname_ Firstname_ac01_ws02_BusinessPlan, replacing Lastname_Firstname with your actual name, and then click **Save**.

d. Click **Slide 1**, if necessary. Replace [Insert name here] with your first and last name. Insert **ac01_ws02_Logo** under your name. Insert a **slide number** at the bottom of every slide except Slide 1.

Figure 39   Business plan title slide

e. Click **Slide 3**, and then type About My Sparkles as the slide title. Click the **text box**, begin with a short description of the industry, and then discuss the present outlook as well as future possibilities. In the second paragraph, provide information on all the various markets within the industry, including any new products or developments that will positively or unfavorably affect your business.

f. Click **Slide 4**, and then type About the Industry as the slide title. Click the **text box**, and then briefly summarize your findings from your Five Forces model. Insert a screenshot of your Five Forces analysis to the right of the text box, and then crop the image so only the Five Forces analysis is visible. Resize the image and text box as needed.

g. Click **Slide 5**, and then type The Specialty Jewelry Industry as the slide title. Click the **text box**, and then discuss the specialty jewelry industry.

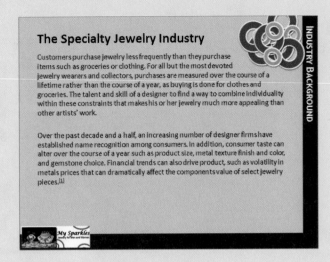

Figure 40   Industry background slide

h. Click **Slide 6**, and then type My Sparkles vs. the Competition as the slide title. Click the **text box**, and then briefly summarize the strengths and weaknesses of the company and industry, as outlined on your SWOT analysis. Insert a screenshot of your SWOT analysis to the right of the text box, and then crop the image so only the SWOT analysis is visible. Resize the image and text box as needed.

i. Click **Slide 7**, and then type Opportunities and Threats as the slide title. Browse to where you are storing your student files, open the **Lastname_Firstname_ac01_ws02_MySparkles** database, and then open **rptDemographicsSalary_initialLastname**. Take a screenshot of the first and last pages of the report, paste them onto Slide 7, and then crop each image so only the report page is visible. Arrange the images so they cascade. Click the **text box**, and then briefly summarize the attractiveness and the changing aspects of the market. Refer to your Five Forces analysis for the opportunities and threats. Resize the image and text box as needed.

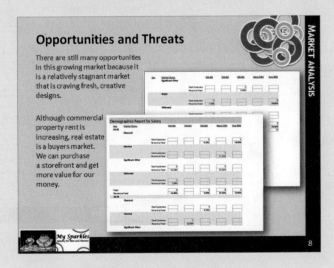

Figure 41   Market analysis slide

j. Click **Slide 8**, and then type Customer Loyalty Program as the slide title. Browse to where you are storing your student files, open **Lastname_Firstname_ac01_ws02_ MySparkles**, and then open **rptDemographicsSalary_initialLastname**. Take a screenshot of the marketing flyer, paste it onto Slide 8, and then crop the image so only the flyer is visible. Resize the image as needed. Click the **text box**, and then briefly summarize the loyalty program. Resize the image and text box as needed.

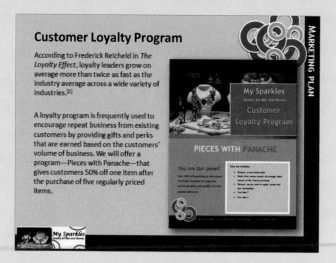

Figure 42   Customer loyalty program slide

k. Click **Slide 9**, and then type Pro-forma Balance Sheet as the slide title. Browse to where you are storing your student files, and then open **Lastname_Firstname_ac01_ws02_ Financials**. Take a screenshot of the pro-forma balance sheet, paste it onto Slide 9, and then crop the image so only the balance sheet is visible. Click the **text box**, and then briefly summarize the financial reports. Resize the image and text box as needed.

l. Duplicate **Slide 9**, and then type Income Statement as the slide title. Delete the proforma balance sheet image. Take a screenshot of the income statement, paste it onto Slide 10, and then crop the image so only the statement is visible. Resize and edit the image as needed.

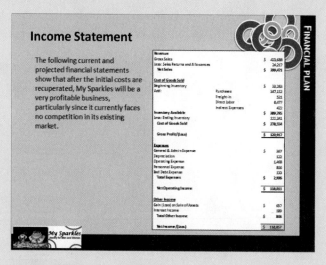

Figure 43   Income statement slide

m. Duplicate **Slide 10**, and then type Cash Flow Statement as the slide title. Delete the income statement image. Take a screenshot of the income statement, paste it onto Slide 11, and then crop the image so only the statement is visible. Resize and edit the image as needed.

n. Click the **File tab**, click **Open**, locate and select **ac01_ws02_OperationsPlan**, and then click **Open**. The operations plan slides should follow Slide 9. Copy and paste the operation plans slides into the business plan presentation and ensure you keep source formatting.

o. Click **Slide 1**, add a new title and content slide, and then type Table of Contents as the slide title and side heading. Using a bulleted list, create a table of contents for your business plan. Remove the slide number from the slide footer.

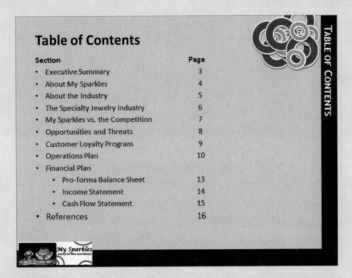

Figure 44   Table of contents slide

p. Click **Slide 3**, and then type an executive summary for your business plan. Use the concepts discussed in the workshop to support your ideas.

q. Click **Slide 16**, and then cite your sources, if necessary. Save your presentation, and then Exit all Office programs.

1. What are the benefits of using a decision support system as a model to help make decisions?

2. What are the pros and cons of using Access over Excel to store and analyze customer and sales data?

3. Compare and contrast SWOT analysis and Porter's Five Forces models.

4. What is the difference between the four P's and the four C's?

5. How can developing a buyer persona assist with marketing to prospective customers?

Key Terms

Asset 47
Balance sheet 44
Business plan 44
Cash flow statement 44
Decision support system (DSS) 45
Demographic segmentation 62
Excel model 45
Five Forces model 72
Income statement 44

Knowledge 51
Liability 47
Liquidity 44
Loyalty program 76
Market segmentation 59
Marketing mix 62
Mass marketing 62
Niche market 62
Niche marketing 62

Persona 67
Pro-forma balance sheet 44
Return on investment (ROI) 79
Startup costs 44
SWOT analysis 69
Target market 59
What-if analysis 45

Visual Summary

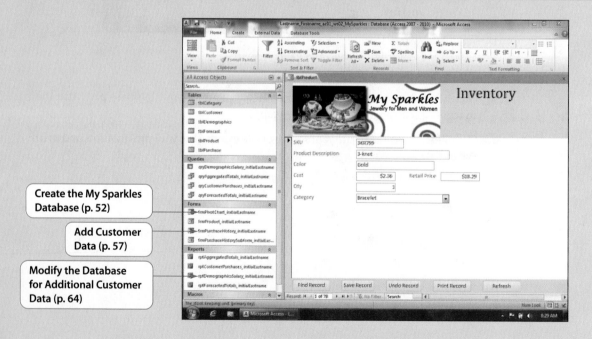

Create the My Sparkles Database (p. 52)

Add Customer Data (p. 57)

Modify the Database for Additional Customer Data (p. 64)

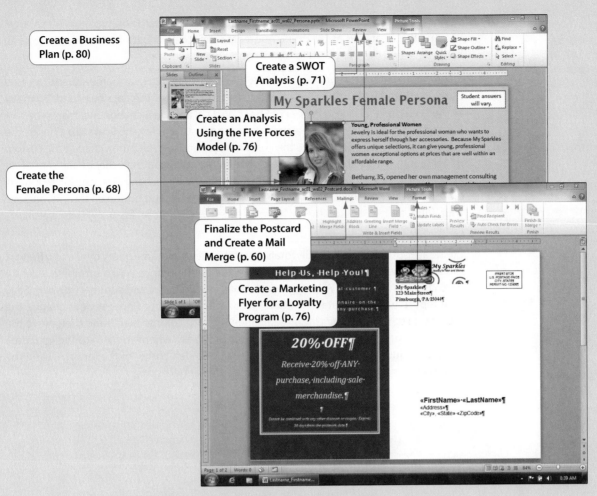

Create a Business Plan (p. 80)

Create a SWOT Analysis (p. 71)

Create an Analysis Using the Five Forces Model (p. 76)

Create the Female Persona (p. 68)

Finalize the Postcard and Create a Mail Merge (p. 60)

Create a Marketing Flyer for a Loyalty Program (p. 76)

Figure 45   Managing Data for an Entrepreneurial Enterprise

Practice 1

Student data files needed:	You will save your files as:
ac01_ws02_MySparkles2	Lastname_Firstname_ac01_ws02_MySparkles2
ac01_ws02_Purchases	Lastname_Firstname_ac01_ws02_Purchases
ac01_ws02_BusinessPlan2	Lastname_Firstname_ac01_ws02_BusinessPlan2
ac01_ws02_Logo	

Applying for a Small Business Loan

Unfortunately, Laura was not approved for a bank loan. Although this is a setback, it is not uncommon for a new business to be denied for a bank loan because the business has no or minimal credit history. Fortunately, the state and federal governments have many loans and grants for small businesses. Laura has asked you to help her update her database so she can retrieve the data easier, export data to Excel to perform data analysis, and then create new slides to add into her business plan.

a. Open the **ac01_ws02_MySparkles2** database. Save it as Lastname_Firstname_ac01_ws02_MySparkles2. Import the new purchases that have occurred since you last worked with the database from **ac01_ws02_Purchases** into the tblPurchase table.

b. Create a new query that includes PurchaseDate from tblPurchase, CategoryName from tblCategory, and Quantity from tblProduct. Aggregate the data by counting the quantity. Rename the Quantity field Total. Save the query as qryDailyTotals_initialLastname. Using the qryDailyTotals_initialLastname query, create a crosstab query that uses PurchaseDate as the row heading, CategoryName as the column heading, and sums the Total field in each column and row intersection. Save the query as qryDailyTotalsCrosstab_initialLastname. Rename the Total field as Quantity. Aggregate the totals in Datasheet view and total all fields. Save and close qryDailyTotalsCrosstab_initialLastname.

c. Create a PivotChart from the qryDailyTotalsCrosstab_initialLastname query. Include **PurchaseDate by Month** as the category field, **Quantity** as the data field, and **Quantity** as the series field. Click the **Property Sheet button**, and then change the chart type to a Stacked Column chart. Click the y-axis value range and then click the **Scale tab**. Change the custom max range to 50, change the custom major unit to 5, and then change the custom minor unit to 1. Click the y-axis title, click the **Format tab**, and then change the caption to Quantity. Click the x-axis title, click the **Format tab** and then change the caption to Month. Close the Properties sheet. Add a legend by clicking the **Legend** button on the Ribbon. Save your form as frmDailyTotalsPivotChart_initialLastname. Close frmDailyTotalsPivotChart_initialLastname.

d. Create a report from the qryDailyTotalsCrosstab_initialLastname query by clicking **Report Wizard** on the Create tab. Include all the fields on the report. Add a grouping level for PurchaseDate by month. Add aggregated totals so the detail and summary display. Save your report as rptDailyTotalsCrosstab_initialLastname. Close Print Preview, change the report title to Daily Totals by Month, change the font color to black, and then move the report title to the center of the report header. Browse to where you are storing your data files and include the **ac01_ws02_Logo** in the upper-left corner of the report. Delete the Text16 text box, and then resize and rename fields as necessary.

Month	Date	Total	Bracelet	Earrings	Moneyclip	Necklace	Ring
January 2013							
	1/2/2013	1		1			
	1/3/2013	4		2			2
	1/5/2013	2				1	1
	1/6/2013	2					2
	1/8/2013	1				1	
	1/9/2013	1		1			
	1/10/2013	1				1	
	1/11/2013	1		1			
	1/12/2013	1					1
	1/13/2013	2	1				1
	1/14/2013	1					1
	1/15/2013	2	1				1
	1/16/2013	1					1
	1/18/2013	1				1	
	1/19/2013	2				1	1
	1/20/2013	1					1
	1/21/2013	1		1			
	1/22/2013	2		1			1
	1/23/2013	1			1		
	1/25/2013	2				1	1
	1/26/2013	1					1
	1/29/2013	1					1

Figure 46   Daily totals by month report

e. Laura would like you to create a navigation form so it is easier for her to navigate the database. Click the **Create** tab, click the **Navigation** button, and then click **Horizontal Tabs**. Close the Field List, if necessary. Replace the Navigation Form text with Welcome to the My Sparkles Database. Include the ac01_ws02_Logo in the upper-left corner of the form. Replace [Add New] on the first tab with frmPivotChart, and then press Enter. Replace [Add New] on the next tab with frmDailyTotalsPivotChart_initialLastname, and then press Enter. Replace [Add New] on the next tab with frmPurchaseHistory, and then press Enter. Replace [Add New] on the next tab with frmProduct, and then press Enter. Replace [Add New] on the next tab with rptAggregatedTotals, and then press Enter. Replace [Add New] on the next tab with rptCustomerPurchases, and then press Enter. Replace [Add New] on the next tab with rptForecastedTotals, and then press Enter.

f. Modify the text that is displayed on each tab. Click the **frmPivotChart** tab, and then click the **Property Sheet** button on the Design tab. Click the **Format tab**, if necessary. Change the caption to Daily Totals Chart. Click the **frmDailyTotalsPivotChart_initialLastname tab**, and then change the caption to Daily Totals PivotChart. Click the **frmPurchaseHistory** tab, and then change the caption to Purchase History. Click the **frmProduct tab**, and then change the caption to Products. Click the **rptAggregatedTotals tab**, and then change the caption to Forecasting. Click the **rptCustomerPurchases tab**, and then change the caption to Purchases. Click the **rptForecastedTotals tab**, and then change the caption to Forecasted Totals. Resize the tabs so all headings can be read. Save your changes.

Figure 47   My Sparkles navigation form

g. Open the **AutoExec macro** in Design view. Edit the form name so the navigation form opens automatically when the database opens. Minimize the Navigation Pane so it does not display when the database is opened. Save your changes, close the macro, and then close Access.

h. Click the **Start** button, and then select **Excel 2010**.

i. Click the **File tab**, click **Open**, locate and select **ac01_ws02_Purchases**, and then click **Open**.

j. Browse to where you are storing your student files. In the File name box, type Lastname_Firstname_ac01_ws02_Purchases, replacing Lastname_Firstname with your actual name and then click **Save**. Insert a PivotTable on a new worksheet. Select **PurchaseDate** and **SKU** as the row labels, and then select **Qty** and **Price** as the values. Click a date in column A, click the **Options tab**, click the **Group Field** button, and then group the data by quarters. Click the **Design tab**, click the **Subtotals** button, and then show the subtotals at the bottom of each group. Replace the Row Labels heading with Quarter. In cell **A1**, type Total Purchases by Quarter, and increase the font to 14 point. Collapse all groups so only the totals by month are displayed. Click the **PivotTable**, if necessary; click the **Options tab**, and then click the **PivotChart** button. Select **Exploded pie in 3D**. Click the **Design tab**, change the chart layout to **Layout 7**, and then move the chart to a new sheet named **PivotChart**. Click the **Layout tab**, and then click **Inside End**. Add a chart title above the layout area, and then type Total Sales by Quarter. Increase the font in the legend to 18 point, and then increase the font in the chart title to 28 point. Increase the font in the data labels to 16 point, and then change the font color to white. Rename Sheet 1 to PivotTable. Save your changes and then close Lastname_Firstname_ac01_ws02_Purchases.

k. Click the **Start** button, and then select **PowerPoint 2010**.

l. Click the **File tab**, click **Open**, locate and select **ac01_ws02_BusinessPlan2**, and then click **Open**. Browse to where you are storing your student files. In the File name box, type Lastname_Firstname_ac01_ws02_BusinessPlan2, replacing Lastname_Firstname with your actual name, and then click **Save**.

m. Laura would like you to create some new slides that can be added to the business plan. Type This Year's Totals as the title. In the side bar heading, type Financial Plan. In the My Sparkles database, take a screenshot of the Daily Totals PivotChart, paste it onto Slide 1, and then crop the image so only the chart is visible. Click the **text box**, and then briefly summarize the current totals. Resize the image and text box as needed.

n. Insert a new Title and Content slide. Type Forecasted Revenue as the title. In the side bar heading, type Financial Plan. In the My Sparkles database, take a screenshot of the Daily Totals Chart, paste it onto Slide 2, and then crop the image so only the chart is visible. Click the **text box**, and then briefly summarize the forecasted revenue. Resize the image and text box as needed.

o. Insert a new Title and Content slide. Type Forecasted Totals as the title. In the side bar heading, type Financial Plan. In the My Sparkles database, take a screenshot of the Financial Plan, paste it onto Slide 3, and then crop the image so only the report is visible. Click the **text box**, and then briefly summarize the forecasted totals. Resize the image and text box as needed, and then close the Lastname_Firstname_ac01_ws02_MySparkles2 database.

p. Click **Slide 1**, and then insert a new Title and Content slide. Type This Year's Totals by Quarter as the title. In the side bar heading, type Financial Plan. In the Lastname_Firstname_ac01_ws02_Purchases workbook, click the **PivotTable tab**, and then modify the formatting of the PivotTable so it matches the colors in the PowerPoint presentation. Take a screenshot of the PivotTable, paste it onto Slide 2, and then crop the image so only the report is visible. Take a screenshot of the PivotChart, paste it onto Slide 2, and then crop the image so only the chart is visible. Click the **text box**, and then briefly summarize the forecasted totals. Resize the images and text box as needed. Save and close the Lastname_Firstname_ac01_ws02_Purchases workbook. Exit all Office programs.

Practice 2

Student data files needed:

ac01_ws02_BusinessPlan3
ac01_ws02_OlderPersona
ac01_ws02_Financials2

You will save your files as:

Lastname_Firstname_ac01_ws02_BusinessPlan3
Lastname_Firstname_ac01_ws02_Financials2

Dealing with a New Competitor in the Marketplace

Now that Laura finally received funding from the Small Business Administration, she has purchased a building and has been open in her new location for five months. Her sales are greater than what she expected, and she is pleased with the results. She recently learned that a competitor is opening in the area and is concerned that it might take some of her business away. She has asked you to help expand the marketing analysis and then create new slides to add into her business plan. Additionally, she will need you to update her income statement to include this year's figures.

a. It has been several months since Laura's business plan was developed, and she would like you to conduct a web search for specialty jewelry shops in the local area. Laura has provided information about the newest competitor, Coletti Designs.

Element	Details
Type of jewelry	An exclusive line of jewelry uniquely designed and hand-crafted by Jenny Coletti.
Consultations	Customer consultations are available upon request.
Materials	Jenny's unique jewelry designs are made with only the highest quality materials including: • Swarovski crystal • Precious and semi-precious stones • Sterling and gold • Natural fiber and beads • Rare vintage beads and brass • Venetian glass
Location	Ten miles from My Sparkles.
Payments accepted	Cash, check, MasterCard, and Visa.
Website	Has web presence, but customers must purchase items only on location.

b. Click the **Start** button, and then select **PowerPoint 2010**.

c. Click the **File tab**, click **Open**, locate and select **ac01_ws02_BusinessPlan3**, and then click **Open**.

d. Browse to where you are storing your student files. In the File name box, type Lastname_Firstname_ac01_ws02_BusinessPlan3, replacing Lastname_Firstname with your actual name, and then click **Save**. Type My Sparkles vs. the Competition as the title. In the side bar heading, type Competitor Analysis. Create a SWOT analysis based on your findings. In the text box, briefly explain your analysis. Include the updated information about My Sparkles.

Element	Details
Type of jewelry	An elite line of jewelry uniquely designed and hand-crafted by Laura Schmidt.
Consultations	Customer consultations are available by appointment or walk-in.
Materials	Laura's unique jewelry designs are made with only the highest quality materials including: • Swarovski crystal • Precious and semi-precious stones • Sterling and gold • Natural fiber and beads • Venetian glass
Location	Central location with high visibility and traffic.
Payments accepted	Cash, check, MasterCard, Visa, Discover, and American Express.
Website	Has no web presence.
Additional notes	Laura has implemented a POS system and uses a computer to manage her business. Her marketing plan is having positive results, but the results are not as great as she expected. Although she now has employees, she is the only one who actually designs jewelry. A large portion of the target market is still unaware of the business; thus, she still has room to grow.

e. Insert a new Title and Content slide. Type My Sparkles Older Woman Persona as the title. In the side bar heading, type Marketing Plan. Laura discovered a new market segmentation. Use the following information along with your own ideas to develop the new persona. Insert **ac01_ws02_OlderPersona**, and then resize the image and text box as needed.

Demographic	Details
Age	50–65 years old
Marital status	Divorced/widowed
Pastimes	Working in her garden, shopping, and spending time with family and friends—especially her grandchildren.
Annual salary	$85,000–$105,000
Highest level of education completed	Four-year college degree
Employment status	Retired

f. Insert a new Title and Content slide. Type Building the Business as the title. In the side bar heading, type Marketing Plan. Based on your SWOT analysis, discuss three methods in which Laura can continue to gain market share. Consider the new business that is coming into the area, Laura's current target market, and new persona. Save your changes and then close **Lastname_Firstname_ac01_ws02_BusinessPlan3**.

g. Click the **Start** button, and then select **Excel 2010**.

h. Click the **File tab**, click **Open**, locate and select **ac01_ws02_Financials2**, and then click **Open**.

i. Browse to where you are storing your student files. In the File name box, type Lastname_Firstname_ac01_ws02_Financials2, replacing Lastname_Firstname with your actual name, and then click **Save**.

j. Use the following data to update the 2014 column. Use formulas, functions, and cell names when necessary. Format the cells according to the formats in column D.

Item	Amount
Gross sales	$382,223
Sales returns and allowances	$12,092
Beginning inventory	Ending inventory from last year
Purchases	$241,005
Freight-in	$330
Direct labor	$7,942
Indirect expenses	$279
Ending inventory	$382,201
General & admin expense	$572
Depreciation	$425
Operating expense	$3,856
Personnel expense	$20,087
Bad debt expense	$72
Gain (Loss) on Sale of Assets	$117,420
Interest income	$648

k. Save your changes and then close **Lastname_Firstname_ac01_ws02_Financials2**. Exit all Office programs.

Student data file needed:

ac01_pf1_Pool_Club

You will save your files as:

Lastname_Firstname_ac01_pf1_Pool_Club

Lastname_Firstname_ac01_pf1_Profit_and_Loss_Statement

Lastname_Firstname_ac01_pf1_Pool_Club_Report

Lastname_Firstname_ac01_pf1_Pool_Club_Presentation

Painted Paradise Pool Membership

Earlier this year, the Painted Paradise Resort marketing manager made a proposal to the resort owners to increase revenues by encouraging the use of resort services by local residents. While spa services and golf were already open to the public, use of the pool was reserved for guests of the hotel. The marketing manager felt that making the pool available to the public would attract families to the resort, which could result in their use of additional resort services and thus generate additional revenue.

The resort owners agreed to let the marketing manager implement the plan for a three-month trial period, after which the plan would be evaluated. There were two main requirements: that the plan is profitable, and that the resort atmosphere is preserved.

The Painted Paradise Pool Club offered two membership types: Individual and Family. Membership fees were $15 for an Individual and $45 for a Family. Family memberships have a designated primary member and one or more associate members, aged 8 and older. Associate members must all live at the same address as the primary member, but it is not necessary for them to have the same last name. Membership cards are issued to all primary and associate members.

To cooperate with Health Department Food Service regulations and to maintain the resort atmosphere, bringing food into the resort from outside was prohibited. The marketing manager was concerned that this might discourage families with young children, so all Pool Club memberships were enrolled in a Snack Bar Loyalty Club program. Each time a member or associate member makes a purchase at one of the four snack bars at the resort, the purchase amount is added to a running total for that membership. Snack Bar Loyalty Program reward levels are calculated at the end of every month. For every $40 spent during the month, the member receives a $2 certificate that can be used toward any resort service. Members also receive a $2 certificate as a "birthday gift" during the month of their birthdate.

At the time that a guest signs up for a membership, membership cards are printed in the main office and inserted in a waterproof plastic cover on a Painted Paradise Resort lanyard. It takes approximately 15 minutes of the Office Administrator's time to accept the membership application and payment, and to issue membership cards. It costs $2.50 for each plastic cover and lanyard.

a. Start Access, and open **ac01_pf1_PoolClub**. Click the Enable Content button if the Security Warning appears. Save the database as Lastname_Firstname_ac01_pf1_Pool_Club.

b. Open each table and familiarize yourself with the fields. Open the Relationships window and note how the tables are related.

c. Create a form with a subform that will allow the staff to enter the membership information for new Pool Club primary and associate members. Change the title to Pool Club Members. Save the form as frmPoolClubMembership.

d. Using frmPoolClubMembership, enter yourself as a member with an Individual membership type. Use your actual name and address; all other data can be fictitious.

e. The marketing manager wants to know how many Pool Club memberships were actually sold, and the income from membership fees. Create a query that displays a count of each membership type and the total membership fees collected for each membership type. Save the query as qryFeeIncomeByMembershipType.

f. The marketing manager would like to know how much money Pool Club members are spending at the resort snack bars. Create a query to display each invoice total. Only invoices for Pool Club members during the three-month trial period from 1/1/2013 to 3/31/2013 should be displayed. Format the invoice total as currency. Add a Total row to Sum the total amount spent by Pool Club members at the snack bar during the trial period. Save the query as qryMemberSalesByInvoice.

g. Total sales are not a measure of profit. Profit is determined by subtracting cost from income. Create a query that calculates the total retail sales income on each item on each member invoice, as well as the total item cost. Be sure to account for multiples of the same item on an invoice. Add Total rows to sum the retail sales and item costs. Save the query as qryItemSalesAndCost.

h. At the end of each month of the Pool Club trial period, loyalty program rewards must be calculated and distributed to Pool Club members. Create a parameter query to calculate the snack bar sales totals by member by month. Save the query as qrySalesByMemberByMonth.

i. Using the previous query, create a query to calculate the number of Snack Bar Loyalty certificates earned by each Pool Club member based on his or her total snack bar purchases for the month. (*Note*: Members cannot receive a partial Snack Bar Loyalty program reward, so if their total purchases for the month were $77, they would be eligible for 1 Loyalty Reward certificate.) Save the query as qrySnackBarLoyaltyCertificatesEarned. (*Hint*: Use the INT() function.)

j. As part of their Pool Club membership benefits, all members received an extra certificate during the month of their birthday. This is an expense that the marketing manager has to account for when calculating the profitability of the Pool Club. Create a query to display the member ID, name, address, and birthdate of each member who had a birthday during the three months of the Pool Club trial. Add a Total row to count the number of members that had a birthday during the trial period. Save the query as qryMemberBirthMonth. (*Hint*: Use the Month() function.)

k. Create another query similar to qryMemberBirthMonth to identify and count the number of associate members who had a birthday during the trial period. Save the query as qryAssociateMemberBirthMonth.

l. Additional expenses of the Pool Club are the time it takes for the Office Administrator to process each membership and the expense of the membership cards and lanyards. Write a query to count the number of members and count the number of associate members. Save the query as qryMembershipCount.

m. One of the requirements of the resort owners was that the Pool Club be profitable. To determine whether this goal has been met, the marketing manager must create a Profit and Loss statement, adding up all income generated by Pool Club members and subtracting the related expenses. This should be done in Excel by exporting all query results from Lastname_Firstname_ac01_pf1_Pool_Club to workbooks and then combining them into one workbook. Create the Profit and Loss statement on a new spreadsheet, using cell references to cells on the supporting spreadsheets in the workbook. With the exception of exported values, all numeric amounts must be calculated in Excel with a formula or function. Save the completed workbook as Lastname_Firstname_ac01_pf1_Profit_and_Loss_Statement.

n. Income includes membership fees and snack bar revenue. Expenses include the cost of employee time to enroll a new member, the cost of membership cards, the cost of Snack Bar Loyalty certificates and birthday certificates, and the cost of snack bar items. Create a Report in Word to display the income and expense details from the profit and loss spreadsheet. Include a cover sheet, table of contents, and supporting documents from Access and Excel. Save the file as Lastname_Firstname_ac01_pf1_Pool_Club_Report.

o. Create a PowerPoint presentation for the resort owners justifying whether the Pool Club membership program should be continued. Save the file as Lastname_Firstname_ac01_pf1_Pool_Club_Presentation. Exit all Office programs.

Perform 2: Perform in Your Career

Student data file needed:

ac01_pf2_Pool_Supplies

You will save your files as:

Lastname_Firstname_ac01_pf2_Pool_Supplies
Lastname_Firstname_ac01_pf2_Annual_Demand
Lastname_Firstname_ac01_pf2_Sales_150_Percent_Above_Average
Lastname_Firstname_ac01_pf2_Customer_Form_Letter
Lastname_Firstname_ac01_pf2_Customer_Letter
Lastname_Firstname_ac01_pf2_Mountain_West_Report (Word)
Lastname_Firstname_ac01_pf2_Mountain_West_Report (PowerPoint)

Mountain West Pool Supplies

Mountain West Pool Supplies is an established company in Santa Fe that has been selling pool supplies for 15 years. The company owner, Martin West, has recognized the changing marketplace with the availability of Internet-based competitors. The business maintains a database in support of its day-to-day operations. The owner wants to utilize the information in the database to improve business performance. The initial areas that the owner has requested to be investigated are determining those products that sell the best, whether the inventory costs are as low as possible, and those customers who have purchased products in the past but have not made purchases recently.

The orders for products are processed by the inventory manager and mailed to the appropriate supplier. Each order takes approximately 30 minutes to be processed. The inventory manager is paid an annual salary of $45,800. The warehouses have a storage capacity of 4,000 cubic feet of the total volume of 7,000 cubic feet. The monthly rent and utility costs of the warehouses are $2,500.00. The labor costs of the warehouse staff are $10.52 per hour for each of four employees working 40 hours per week.

a. Start Access, and open ac01_pf2_Pool_Supplies. Save the database as Lastname_Firstname_ac01_pf2_Pool_Supplies.

b. Open each table and familiarize yourself with the fields. Add yourself as a customer to the tblCustomer table. Open the Relationships window and note how the tables are related. Close all tables and the Relationships window.

c. Create the queries to identify the products that have had total sales in May 2013 greater than 150% of the average total monthly sales for that product. Save your query as qrySales150PercentAboveAverage. Export the results to Excel, and create a chart of these products and a chart of categories of products as appropriate. Name your Excel file Lastname_Firstname_ac01_pf2_Sale_150_Percent_Above_Average.

d. Create the queries to determine the average monthly demand for each product. Export the results to Excel, and compute the Economic Order Quantity and Reorder Point for each product. Name your Excel file Lastname_Firstname_ac01_pf2_Annual_Demand. Close Excel.

e. Create a query of customer purchases for the month of May 2013. Save your query as qryCustomerOrdersMay2013. Close your query. Use this query to identify those customers who have not made a purchase during the month of May 2013. Save your query as qryCustomerWithoutMay2013Orders. Close your query.

f. Develop a mail merge Word document to offer the customers who have not made a purchase during the month of May 2013 a 10% discount on purchase of a popular product if made by the end of June 2013 if they bring the letter to the store or place a phone order. (*Hint*: A popular product is a product that has had total sales greater than 150% of the average total monthly sales for that product.) Name your Word mail merge form document Lastname_Firstname_ac01_pf2_Customer_Form_Letter. Name your Word letter document Lastname_Firstname_ac01_pf2_Customer_Letter.

g. Develop a report on the recommended solutions. Include query results from Access. Include charts from Excel. Include computed results from Excel. Name your Word report document Lastname_Firstname_ac01_pf2_Mountain_West_Report.

h. Develop a PowerPoint presentation based on the report. Include query results from Access. Include charts from Excel. Include computed results from Excel. Name your PowerPoint presentation file Lastname_Firstname_ac01_pf2_Mountain_West_Report.

Perform 3: How Others Perform

Student data files needed:

ac01_pf3_Financials3
ac01_pf3_Cupcakes
ac01_pf3_Logo2
ac01_pf3_BusinessPlan4

You will save your files as:

Lastname_Firstname_ac01_pf3_Financials3
Lastname_Firstname_ac01_pf3_Cupcakes
Lastname_Firstname_ac01_pf3_BusinessPlan4

The Popular Market of Cupcake Bakeries

Jo Jo's Cupcakery is joining the newest, most popular sweets industry of cupcake bakeries. The owners, Joe and Susan Lamar, began this business in their own kitchen and once the word spread regarding their cupcakes, they realized that they had a real business venture before them. They also knew that there is no way they can continue running this business out of their kitchen. They need to acquire funding so they can continue building their business. Thus, they need to develop a business plan that will be used when applying for a bank loan, create a financial analysis of current and forecasted sales trends, and modify their database in order to help manage customers and transactions. Furthermore, they need to analyze the market to make certain that the target market is large enough to sustain the business.

a. Click the **Start** button, and then select **Excel 2010**. Click the **File tab**, click **Open**, locate and select **ac01_pf3_Financials3**, and then click **Open**. Browse to where you are storing your student files. In the File name box, type Lastname_Firstname_ac01_pf3_Financials3, replacing Lastname_Firstname with your actual name, and then click **Save**.

b. Click the **Pro-forma Balance Sheet worksheet tab**, if necessary. Use a function or formula to calculate the totals in cells B13, B16, B17, B24, B27, and B28. Apply the Accounting format to the first number under each subheading and each number in the total sections. Apply Comma formatting to all other numbers and then remove all decimals in column B. Resize columns A and B so all data are visible. In cells B17 and B28, apply conditional formatting so negative numbers will display as red text.

c. Click the **Income Statement worksheet tab**. Assign an appropriate name to cells D10, D19, D29, D31, D36, and D38. Use a formula or function to calculate the totals in cells D10, D19, D21, D29, D31, D36, and D38; apply bold and Accounting formats to the cells; and then apply conditional formatting so negative numbers will display as red text. In cell D38, apply conditional formatting so a positive number will display as Green Fill with Dark Green Text. Apply the Accounting format to the first number in the revenue and expenses sections, apply Comma formatting to all other numbers and then remove all decimals in column D. Resize columns A:D so all data are visible.

d. Click the **Cash Flow Statement worksheet tab**. Reference the appropriate cells on the Income Statement and Pro-forma Balance Sheet worksheets to insert values into column C, and then type 0 for values that are unavailable. Calculate the increase in inventory by subtracting ending inventory from the beginning inventory located on the Income Statement worksheet. Use a formula or function to calculate the totals in cells C16 and C21, apply bold and Accounting formats to the cells, and then apply conditional formatting so negative numbers will display as red text. Apply the Accounting format to number in cell C8, apply Comma formatting to all numbers that have no formatting, and then remove all decimals in column C. Resize columns A:C so all data are visible. Save Lastname_Firstname_ac01_ws02_Financials3.

e. Joe designed a database to track employees and employee training, but it needs to be modified to track customers, products, and purchases. Click the **Start** button, and then select **Access 2010**. Click the **File tab**, click **Open**, locate and select **ac01_pf3_Cupcakes**, and then click **Open**. Browse to where you are storing your student files. In the File name box, type Lastname_Firstname_ac01_pf3_Cupcakes, replacing Lastname_Firstname with your actual name, and then click **Save**.

f. Design a table to store customer data. Create appropriate fields that will describe the customers, and then assign a field to be the primary key. For all fields, enter appropriate data type descriptions, field sizes, and other field properties as needed. Save your table as tblCustomer. Be sure to add a field that stores which employee served the customer. Import data from the Customers worksheet into the tblCustomer table from the **ac01_pf3_CupcakesData** workbook. Be sure to resize fields as needed so all data are visible. Close tblCustomer.

g. Design a table to store products using the following details. For all fields, enter appropriate field sizes, captions, and other field properties as needed. Save your table as tblProducts. Import data from the Customers worksheet into the tblProduct table from the **ac01_pf3_CupcakesData** workbook. Be sure to resize fields as needed so all data are visible. Close tblProduct.

Field	Data Type	Description
CupcakeID	AutoNumber	The cupcake ID (primary key)
CupcakeName	Text	The cupcake name
Flavor	Text	Main flavor of cupcake
Cost	Currency	The manufacturing cost
RetailPrice	Currency	The retail price

h. Design a table to store purchase data. Create appropriate fields that will describe the customer purchases, and then assign a field to be the primary key. For all fields, enter appropriate data type descriptions, field sizes, and other field properties as needed. Save your table as tblPurchase. Import data from the Purchases worksheet into the tblPurchase table from the **ac01_pf3_CupcakesData** workbook. Be sure to resize fields as needed so all data are visible. Close tblPurchase. Open the relationships window and then edit the relationships so the new tables are related to each other or other tables within the database.

PurchaseID	CustomerID	Date	Qty	EmployeeID	CupcakeID	Click to Add
PID01	C011	5/18/2013	6	Aphrodite	Chocolate Chip	
PID02	C05	8/1/2013	1	Tana	Peanut Butter	
PID03	C05	5/12/2013	2	Molly	Mocha	
PID04	C07	4/22/2013	11	Molly	Devil's Food	
PID05	C019	5/22/2013	6	Gwendolyn	Devil's Food	
PID06	C015	8/2/2013	8	Ulric	Coconut	
PID07	C016	6/20/2013	1	Ulric	Chocolate Chip	
PID08	C014	4/10/2013	5	Nomlanga	Coconut	
PID09	C02	4/10/2013	1	Regina	Strawberry Crème	
PID010	C010	5/14/2013	1	Denton	Strawberry Crème	
PID011	C04	6/24/2013	5	Haviva	Strawberry Crème	
PID012	C027	9/5/2013	5	Molly	Strawberry Crème	
PID013	C08	5/24/2013	2	Denton	Chocolate Chip	
PID014	C028	4/15/2013	11	Gwendolyn	Coconut	
PID015	C03	8/30/2013	10	Hadley	Mocha	
PID016	C025	9/1/2013	5	Hadley	Peanut Butter	
PID017	C08	4/8/2013	12	Hadley	Strawberry Crème	
PID018	C014	8/13/2013	5	Aphrodite	Chocolate Chip	
PID019	C01	5/20/2013	8	Aphrodite	Peanut Butter	
PID020	C09	6/30/2013	8	Tana	Mocha	
PID021	C02	5/26/2013	9	Molly	Devil's Food	
PID022	C09	6/4/2013	7	Molly	Devil's Food	
PID023	C025	6/16/2013	9	Gwendolyn	Coconut	
PID024	C031	8/4/2013	10	Ulric	Chocolate Chip	
PID025	C023	5/22/2013	3	Ulric	Coconut	

Lookup field used to display employee's first name

Lookup field used to display the cupcake name

Figure 1 Jo Jo's Cupcakery purchase table

i. Create the following so Joe and Susan can manage their business.

- Create a query using data from tblProduct and tblPurchase that calculates the gross revenue for each type of cupcake sold. Group by CupcakeName, and then sum the Qty and Gross Revenue fields. In Datasheet view, aggregate the totals for the Qty and Gross Revenue fields. Rename and format fields appropriately, and then resize the fields so all data are visible. Save your query as qryGrossRevenue_initialLastname.

- Create a form from the tblCustomer table. Add all the fields to your form. Browse to where you are storing your data files and include the ac01_pf3_Logo2 in the upper-left corner of the form. Add a subform that allows you to view all the purchases that each customer has made. Ensure that the heading, field names, and colors are appropriate; resize fields as needed so all data are visible; and then rename and format fields as necessary. Save your form as frmCustomer_initialLastname and your subform as frmPurchaseHistory_initialLastname. Close frmCustomer_initialLastname.

- Create a PivotChart from the qryGrossRevenue_initialLastname query that displays the gross revenue by cupcake name. Ensure that the axis headings and colors are appropriate. Click the **Drop Zones** button on the Design tab to hide the drop zones that are not in use. Save your PivotChart as frmPivotChartRevenue_initialLastname, and then close frmPivotChartRevenue_initialLastname.

- Create a PivotChart Report from the qryGrossRevenue_initialLastname query that displays the quantity by cupcake name. Ensure that the axis headings and colors are appropriate. Click the **Drop Zones** button on the Design tab to hide the drop zones that are not in use. Save your PivotChart as frmPivotChartQuantity_initialLastname, and then close frmPivotChartQuantity_initialLastname.

- Create a report that lists purchases by month. Include the purchase date and quantity from the tblPurchase table, and then include cupcake name, flavor, and price from the tblProducts table. View your data by tblPurchase. Group the data by the purchase date. Include group and grand total for quantity. Save your report as rptCustomerPurchases_initialLastname. Browse to where you are storing your data files and include the ac01_pf3_Logo2 in the upper-left corner of the report. Ensure that the heading, field names, and colors are appropriate; resize fields as needed so all data are visible; and then rename and format fields as necessary. Close rptCustomerPurchases_initialLastname.

- Create a navigation form so it is easier for Joe and Susan to navigate the database. Replace the Navigation Form text with Welcome to Jo Jo's Cupcakery Database. Add your forms and report to the navigation form. Modify the text that is displayed on each tab so it is easier to understand what is being viewed. Resize the tabs so all headings can be read. Save your form as frmNavigationForm_initialLastname. Create a macro that displays the navigation form when the database opens, and then hide the navigation pane so it does not display. Close Access.

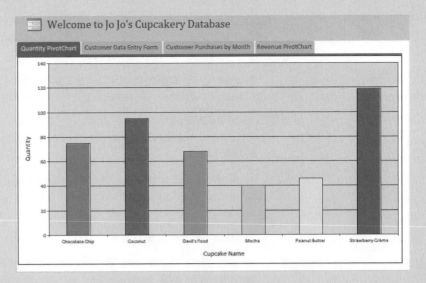

Figure 2 Jo Jo's Cupcakery navigation form

j. Click the **Start** button, and then select **PowerPoint 2010**. Click the **File tab**, click **Open**, locate and select **ac01_pf3_BusinessPlan4**, and then click **Open**. Browse to where you are storing your student files. In the File name box, type Lastname_Firstname_ac01_ pf3_BusinessPlan4, replacing Lastname_Firstname with your actual name, and then click **Save**.

k. Create the following for Jo Jo's Cupcakery business plan. Joe and Susan have added some of the information for you. Be sure to use screenshots where necessary, and then resize images and text boxes as needed. Click **Slide 1**, if necessary. Replace [Insert name here] with your first and last name. Insert a slide number at the bottom of every slide, and then remove the slide number from the slide footer on Slide 1.

l. Click **Slide 5**, and then type About the Industry as the slide title. Research the cupcake bakery industry and then provide an overview of the industry background. Conduct a business environment analysis using the Five Forces model and insert it on Slide 5. Click the **text box**, and then briefly summarize your findings from your Five Forces analysis. Insert your Five Forces analysis to the right of the text box, and then resize the text box as needed.

m. Click **Slide 6**, and then type The Cupcake Bakery Industry as the slide title. Research the cupcake bakery industry, click the **text box**, and then discuss your findings.

n. Click **Slide 7**, and then type Jo Jo's Cupcakery vs. the Competition as the slide title. Using the SWOT model, perform a competitor analysis. Click the **text box**, and then briefly summarize the strengths and weaknesses of the company and industry, as outlined on your SWOT analysis. Resize the text box as needed.

o. Click **Slide 8**, and then type Opportunities and Threats as the slide title. Perform a market analysis using the industry opportunities and threats and then provide an overview of your findings.

p. Joe and Susan have determined that the target market is the middle-aged woman. Click **Slide 9**, and then type Marketing to Customers as the slide title. Based on your SWOT analysis, discuss three marketing plan methods in which Joe and Susan can continue to gain market share.

q. Click **Slide 10**, and then type Pro-forma Balance Sheet as the slide title. Click the **text box**, and then briefly summarize the financial reports. Include a screenshot of the pro-forma balance sheet, crop and resize the image, and then resize text box as needed.

r. Click **Slide 11**, and then type Income Statement as the slide title. Click the **text box**, and then briefly summarize the financial reports. Include a screenshot of the income statement, crop and resize the image, and then resize text box as needed.

s. Click **Slide 12**, and then type Cash Flow Statement as the slide title. Include a screenshot of the cash flow statement, crop and resize the image, and then resize text box as needed.

t. Insert a new slide after Slide 12, and then type Current Data as the slide title. Include charts from the Lastname_Firstname_ac01_pf3_Cupcakes database, and then briefly summarize the items you added.

u. Click **Slide 2**, and then type Business Plan Layout as the slide title. Using a bulleted list, create a table of contents for your business plan. Remove the slide number from the slide footer.

v. Click **Slide 3**, and then type Executive Summary as the slide title. Write an executive summary for your business plan. Use the concepts discussed in the workshop to support your ideas.

w. Click **Slide 14**, and then cite your sources, if necessary.

x. Save and close **Lastname_Firstname_ac01_pf3_BusinessPlan4**, close **Lastname_Firstname_a01_pf3_Financials3**, and then close **Lastname_Firstname_a01_pf3_Cupcakes**. Exit all Office programs.

Perform 4: Perform in Your Career

Student data files needed:	You will save your files as:
ac01_pf4_DinerDatabase	Lastname_Firstname_a01_pf4_DinerDatabase
a01_pf4_DinerLogo	Lastname_Firstname_a01_pf4_DinerFinancials
ac01_pf4_DinerFinancials	Lastname_Firstname_a01_pf4_DinerBusinessPlan
Blank PowerPoint Presentation	

Purchasing a Failing Diner with Tremendous Potential

You are the new owner of Tom's Diner, a 20-year-old local diner that specializes in home-cooked meals for breakfast, lunch, and dinner. In previous years, the diner was very profitable. However, the former owner has not responded well to local competition and has also accrued a great deal of debt. The diner needs to be renovated and you need to market the cook's excellent homemade food to your target market. You may need to acquire funding so you can build the business through renovations and marketing.

The former owner has given you a database that he started using, but never kept it updated. The database includes the diner's inventory, menu items, suppliers, and sales. The former owner has also given you last year's financial statements, which include a pro-forma balance sheet, income statement, and cash flow statement. You need to develop a business plan that will be used when applying for a bank loan; determine forecasted sales trends based on the existing financial data; and append queries, forms, and reports to the database in order to help manage the business. Furthermore, you need to develop ideas that will be used to promote your grand reopening.

a. Click the **Start** button, and then select **Excel 2010**. Click the **File tab**, click **Open**, locate and select **ac01_pf4_DinerFinancials**, and then click **Open**. Browse to where you are storing your student files. In the File name box, type Lastname_Firstname_ac01_pf4_DinerFinancials, replacing Lastname_Firstname with your actual name, and then click **Save**.

b. Click the **Pro-forma Balance Sheet worksheet tab**, if necessary. Notice the relationship between the total assets and total liabilities. For example, the former owner accrued over $76,000 in outstanding debt and the majority of that debt is in accounts payable and short-term notes. Click the **Income Statement worksheet tab**. The former owner's expenses are far greater than the amount of money that is coming into the diner.

c. Click the **Cash Flow Statement worksheet tab**. You believe that you can increase revenue and decrease expenses. Thus, to forecast financials for the next two years, add the following data in range D:E, and then use a formula or function to calculate the missing values in range D:E. Apply the same formatting in range D:E that was used in column C. Save your changes.

Category	2013	2014
Net Income	100,000	250,000

d. Click the **Start** button, and then select **Access 2010**. Click the **File tab**, click **Open**, locate and select **ac01_pf4_DinerDatabase**, and then click **Open**. Browse to where you are storing your student files. In the File name box, type Lastname_Firstname_ac01_pf4_DinerDatabase, replacing Lastname_Firstname with your actual name, and then click **Save**.

e. Create the following so you can easily manage your business.

- Create a query using data from tblSales and tblMenuItems that calculates the gross revenue for each menu item sold. The menu price is three times the food cost. Group by MenuID, and then sum the Gross Revenue field. Sort the Gross Revenue field in descending order to find your highest grossing item. Format Gross Revenue as currency with zero decimals. In Datasheet view, aggregate the totals for the Gross Revenue field. Resize the fields so all data are visible. Save your query as qryGrossRevenue_initialLastname.

- Create a query using data from tblMenuItems that counts the total menu items within each category. Group by Category, and then count the MenuItem field. In Datasheet view, aggregate the totals for the menu items to view how many items currently exist on the menu. Resize the fields so all data are visible. Save your query as qryCategoryTotals_initialLastname.

- Create a form from the tblMenuItems table. Add all the fields to your form. Browse to where you are storing your data files and include the ac01_pf4_DinerLogo in the upper-left corner of the form. Add a subform that allows you to view all the ingredients that are needed to make each menu item. Ensure that the heading, field names, and colors are appropriate; resize fields as needed so all data are visible; and then rename and format fields as necessary. Save your form as frmMenuItems_initialLastname and your subform as frmIngredients_initialLastname. In the form footer, add five control buttons that will help you navigate the form. Add a field that calculates the menu price for each item, and then format the field as currency with zero decimals. Save your changes and then close frmCustomer_initialLastname.

- Create a PivotChart from the qryCategoryTotals_initialLastname query that displays the total menu items within each category. Click the **Drop Zones** button on the Design tab to hide the drop zones that are not in use. Save your PivotChart as frmPivotChartTotals_initialLastname, and then close frmPivotChartTotals_initialLastname.

- Create a report from **qryGrossRevenue_initialLastname**. Save your report as rptGrossRevenue_initialLastname. Browse to where you are storing your data files and include the ac01_pf4_DinerLogo in the upper-left corner of the report. Ensure that the heading, field names, and colors are appropriate, resize fields as needed so all data are visible, and then rename and format fields as necessary. Close rptGrossRevenue_initialLastname.

- Create a report from **qryCategoryTotals_initialLastname**. Save your report as rptCategoryTotals_initialLastname. Browse to where you are storing your data files and include the ac01_pf4_DinerLogo in the upper-left corner of the report. Ensure that the heading, field names, and colors are appropriate; resize fields as needed so all data are visible; and then rename and format fields as necessary. Close rptCategoryTotals_initialLastname.

- Create a navigation form so it is easier for you to navigate the database. Replace the Navigation Form text with Welcome to the Tom's Diner Database. Add your forms and reports to the navigation form. Modify the text that is displayed on each tab so it is easier to understand what is being viewed. Resize the tabs so all headings can be read. Save your form as **frmNavigationForm_initialLastname**. Create a macro that displays the navigation form when the database opens, and then hide the Navigation Pane so it does not display. Save and then close your macro.

f. Click the Start button, and then select **PowerPoint 2010**. Browse to where you are storing your student files. In the File name box, type Lastname_Firstname_ac01_pf4_DinerBusinessPlan, replacing Lastname_Firstname with your actual name, and then click Save. Begin by creating a template that can be used for your business plan. Use appropriate graphics and colors, and then include the diner logo in the appropriate places. Be sure to use screenshots where necessary, and then resize images and text boxes as needed.

g. Create a title slide. Include your first and last name, and then include the company name. Type Serving Homemade Food for Over 20 Years as the subheading.

h. Insert a new slide, type Business Environment Analysis as the side title and then type About the Industry as the slide title. Research the restaurant industry and then provide an overview of the industry background. Conduct a business environment analysis using the Five Forces model, insert it on the slide, and then resize the text box as needed.

i. Insert a new slide, type Industry Background as the side title, and then type The Diner History as the slide title. Research the history of diners, click the text box, and then discuss your findings.

j. Insert a new slide, type Competitor Analysis as the side title, and then type Tom's Diner vs. the Competition as the slide title. Using the SWOT model, perform a competitor analysis. Click the **text box**, and then briefly summarize the strengths and weaknesses of the company and industry as outlined on your SWOT analysis. Resize the text box as needed.

k. You have determined that the target market is the young family. Insert a new slide, type Market Analysis as the side title, and then type Marketing to Customers as the slide title. Based on your SWOT analysis, discuss three marketing plan methods that you can implement to gain market share.

l. Insert a new slide, type Financial Analysis as the side title, and then type Pro-forma Balance Sheet as the slide title. Click the **text box**, and then briefly summarize the financial reports. Include a screenshot of the pro-forma balance sheet, crop and resize the image, and then resize text box as needed.

m. Insert a new slide, type Financial Analysis as the side title, and then type Income Statement as the slide title. Click the **text box**, and then briefly summarize the financial reports. Include a screenshot of the income statement, crop and resize the image, and then resize text box as needed.

n. Insert a new slide, type Financial Analysis as the side title, and then type Cash Flow Statement as the slide title. Click the **text box,** and then briefly summarize the financial reports. Include a screenshot of the cash flow statement, crop and resize the image, and then resize text box as needed.

o. Insert a new slide, type Financial Analysis as the side title, and then type Current Data as the slide title. Include the PivotChart from the Lastname_Firstname_ac01_pf4_DinerDatabase database. Briefly summarize the item you added, and then explain how menu item prices are calculated.

p. Insert a new slide after Slide 1, type Table of Contents as the side title, and then type Business Plan Layout as the slide title. Using a bulleted list, create a table of contents for your business plan.

q. Insert a new slide after Slide 1, and then type Executive Summary as the slide title. Write an executive summary for your business plan. Use the concepts discussed in the workshop to support your ideas.

r. Insert a new slide at the end of the presentation, and then cite your sources, if necessary. Insert a slide number at the bottom of every slide, and then do not show the slide number on the title slide.

s. Save and close **Lastname_Firstname_a01_pf4_DinerBusinessPlan**, close **Lastname_Firstname_a01_pf4_Financials4**, and then close **Lastname_Firstname_a01_pf4_DinerDatabase**. Exit all Office programs.

Glossary

A

ABS( )—An intrinsic function that converts the value passed to the unsigned equivalent value.

Asset—An object you own that holds value, such as cash, stock, inventory, property rights, and goodwill.

B

Balance sheet—This illustrates the outflow and inflow of cash over a certain period of time. One side shows the organization's assets and liabilities, while the other side shows how they are financed. The two sides must match in value, or "balance."

Business plan—This is a formal statement that summarizes forecasted—usually one to three years—operational and financial objectives and explains how they will be achieved.

Business problem—A situation that is an obstacle to achieving a business goal, such as increasing revenue, increasing profits, reducing costs, or improving productivity.

C

Cash flow statement—A financial statement that indicates how changes in balance sheet accounts and revenue affect cash and cash equivalents, and then breaks the analysis down to operating, investing, and financing activities.

D

Data anomalies—These occur when the data value for an entity appears twice in different locations—tables—and those two data values are not the same.

Data redundancy—The multiple appearances of a data value in the tables of a database.

Decision support system—An information system that supports managerial decision-making activities by representing a problem, either mathematically or symbolically, that a manager needs to solve.

Demand—The number of products that are expected to be sold to customers over a unit of time.

Demographic segmentation—The most popular method for separating groups, primarily because consumer needs usually match demographic categories, but also because demographic variables are relatively easy to obtain and measure.

E

Economic order quantity (EOQ)—The optimum quantity to order of a product that will result in the minimum total inventory cost.

Excel model—An Excel model includes a series of equations, input factors, parameters, and variables that are used to solve the problem at hand.

F

Five Forces model—In 1979, Michael E. Porter of Harvard Business School developed the Five Forces model to use as a framework for industry analysis and business strategy development. The model is used to determine the competitive power and consequently the attractiveness of a market.

FIX( )—An intrinsic function that converts the value passed to a whole number by dropping any decimal portion.

H

Holding cost—The cost to store and maintain a product in inventory for a unit of time.

I

Income statement—Also referred to in business as a statement of profit and loss, it itemizes past revenues and expenses that caused the current profit or loss, and indicates what may be done to improve the results.

INT( )—An intrinsic function that converts the value passed to the nearest integer value.

Intrinsic function—A programmed calculation included in a software application that performs a common process.

Inventory—Products stored and maintained for sale to customers.

K

Knowledge—This is applied information once you make a decision.

L

LEFT( )—An intrinsic function that determines the string of characters from the string that is the first argument that makes up the first N characters starting from the left side of the string argument. N is a whole number that is the second argument to the function.

Liability—An item that someone is legally responsible for, such as an obligation, responsibility, or debt.

Liquidity—The ability to quickly convert assets such as money market accounts, bonds, or Treasury bills to cash.

Loyalty program—This is frequently used to encourage repeat business from existing customers by providing gifts and perks that are earned based on the volume of business your customers do with you.

M

Mail Merge—A process of creating one or more documents or e-mail messages by combining data values from a data source with a form document or e-mail message that individualizes the content of each document or e-mail message.

Market segmentation—A result of learning that all prospective customers are not alike, and that the same general appeal will not interest all prospects.

Marketing mix—This is vital when determining a product or brand's unique selling point and is frequently synonymous with the "four Ps": price, product, promotion, and place.

Mass marketing—When an organization decides to overlook market segment differences and aim for selling to the whole market by focusing on high sales and low prices.

N

Niche market—A niche market, such as Rolls Royce and Bentley Motors, has a narrowly defined group of potential customers.

Niche marketing—These companies address a need for a product or service that is not being addressed by conventional suppliers.

Normalized—A database that includes the natural relationships that exist among the entities—customers, sales, employees, inventory, and suppliers.

O

Order cost—The cost to develop an order of a product. This does not include the cost of the product.

P

Persona—A fictional character that is generated to represent the customers within a targeted demographic and is primarily developed to help determine where there are opportunities and areas for improvement.

Planning steps—The steps that are followed to develop the solution to a problem. The steps are: defining the problem; identifying what you know and need to know to solve the problem; developing the solution; and documenting and presenting your solution and/or recommendation(s).

Pro-forma balance sheet—This displays similar information, but also illustrates events that have happened during the period of time in which the balance sheet had been created. This permits people within the organization to identify trends more easily and predict the cash position they will have at a specific point in time.

R

Relationship—The linking of two tables in a database using a common field in both tables.

Reorder point—The current inventory quantity of a product when a new order should be placed so that the order will arrive when the last product is sold.

Return on investment—This is a method used to measure performance and evaluates whether an investment will pay for itself or help generate more revenue. To calculate ROI, the benefit (return) of an investment is divided by the cost of the investment—the result is expressed as a percentage or a ratio.

ROUND( )—An intrinsic function that converts the value passed as the first argument to the value to the nearest digit using the precision passed as the second argument.

S

SQR( )—An intrinsic function in Access that computes the square root of the value passed as an argument.

SQRT( )—An intrinsic function in Excel that computes the square root of the value passed as an argument.

Startup costs—These are fixed costs associated with starting a business. These costs are often non-reoccurring costs such as legal fees, advertising fees, promotional activity fees, and employee training.

SWOT analysis—A strategic planning technique used to evaluate the Strengths, Weaknesses, Opportunities, and Threats involved in a project or business venture.

T

Target market—A group of people that the business has decided to focus its marketing efforts and eventually its merchandise toward.

W

What-if analysis—The process of changing the values in certain cells to see how those changes will affect the outcome of formulas or functions on the worksheet.

Index

3-D clustered column charts, 17–18

3D exploded pie charts, 55

A

ABS( ) function, **10**

absolute references, 25

Access

    available functions in, 9

    charting vs. Excel charting, 66

    databases, 51

    exporting data for Excel analysis, charting, 16–19

    starting, 4

Accounting format, 49

adding

    fields to queries, 8

    logos to reports, 54

    subforms, 58

    worksheets to workbooks, 65–66

aggregated subqueries, creating, 53

Armstrong, Gary, 63

assets, **47**

AutoCorrect Options, 25

B

balance sheet, **44**

bargaining power of buyers, 74

Borden, Neil, 62

business plans, **44**

    compiling, 77

    components of, 78–80

    conducting SWOT analyses of, 71

business problems

    defining, 2–3, 27–28

    described, **2**

buyers, bargaining power of, 74

C

calculated fields, 30

    adding, 57–58

    creating, 11, 16

captions, and reserved words (Access), 56

cases

    Golf Nook Clothing Store, 1

    My Sparkles jewelry company, 43

cash flow statements, **44**

    creating, 49–50

    using, 47–48

charting percentages of products, 17–19

charts

    changing to 3-D exploded pie chart, 55

    in Excel vs. Access, 66

checking formulas, 25

coloring data point columns, 17–18

Comma formatting, 25, 49

communication (four C's), 63

Competitive strategy: Techniques for analyzing industries and competitors (Porter), 72

conditional formatting, 49, 54

Confirm Data Source dialog box, 34

consumer (four C's), 63

convenience (four C's), 63

cost (four C's), 63

cover pages, adding to reports, 26

creating

    business plans, 44–50, 77–83

    calculated fields, 11

    cash flow statements, 49–50

    chart of sorted data, 17–19

    crosstab queries, 64–65

    customer analysis report, presentation, 27–35

    customer loyalty programs, 76–77

    database tables, 56–58

    databases, 51–56

    e-mail messages, 32

expressions, 53

Five Forces model analysis, 72–76

forms, 55

income statements, 48

inventory analysis report, 26–27

letters, 33–34

Mail Merge, 60–61

marketing flyers, 76–77

personas, 67–69

PivotChart forms, 55

presentations, 35, 80–83

pro-forma balance sheet, 47–48

queries, 53–54

queries of month's sales, 8–10

query of annual demand by product, 23

query of annual sales by product, 24

query of cumulative sales, 13–14

query of current inventory, 11–12

query of customers who purchased, 28–31

query of percentage of starting inventory sold in month, 15–16

query of starting inventory, 14–15

relationships, 4–7, 23, 52

reports, 53–54, 57–58, 65

reports of problem solution, 19–27

SWOT analyses, 69–71, 71

crosstab queries, creating, 64–65

Currency format, 25

current assets, 47

current liabilities, 47

customer data

managing, 59

working with, 56–58

customers

creating loyalty programs, 76–77

soliciting feedback from, 69

CVS Caremark, 60

D

data

customer, 56–59

exporting for Excel analysis, charting, 16–19

exporting to Excel for analysis and calculations, 24–25

data anomalies, **3**

data files

needed for Workshop 1, 1

needed for Workshop 2, 43

data redundancy, **3**

data types, matching, 5–6

database tables

creating, 56–58

importing worksheet data into, 64

databases

creating, 51–56

Golf Nook, 3

queries. *See* queries

updating, 64–66

Datasheet view, 4, 9

decision support system (DSS), **45**

demand, **21**

demographic segmentation, **62**

Design view, 8, 30

DSS (decision support system), **45**

E

economic order quantity (EOQ), **22**

e-mail

addresses, creating queries using, 29–30

messages, creating, 32

errors

in expressions, 10

in queries, 30

Excel

charting vs. Access charting, 66

exporting Access data for analysis, charting, 16–19

importing data for analysis and calculations, 24–25

vs. relational databases, 51

Excel model, **45**

executive summaries in business plans, 79–80

Export-Excel Spreadsheet Wizard, 16, 24–25

exporting

data for Excel analysis, charting, 16–19

data to Excel for analysis and calculations, 24–25

Expression Builder, 10, 30

expressions, creating, 53

F

fields

adding to queries, 8

creating calculated, 11

lookup, 64

financial analyses, performing, 45–50

Five Forces model

analyzing industries using, 72–76

described, **72**

FIX( ) function, **10**

fixed assets, 47

forecasting sales, 46

Format Painter, 25

formatting

business plans, 78

conditional, 49, 54

percent values, 16

forms

creating, 55, 58

saving, 58

formulas, checking, 25

four C's, 62–63

four P's, 62

functions

available in Access, 9

intrinsic, **9**

G

Golf Nook Clothing Store (case), 1

H

holding cost, **21**

Humphrey, Albert, 69

I

importing worksheet data into database
table, 64

income statements, 47–48

creating, 48

described, **44**

using in presentation, 82

INT( ) function, **10**

intrinsic functions

common math (fig.), 10

described, **9**

inventory, **2**, 43

analysis report, creating, 26–27

creating query of annual demand by
product, 23

creating query of current, 11–12

creating query of starting, 14–15

planning analysis, 21–22

starting, 12

J

Jackson, Thomas Penfield, 74

jewelry industry, 71

K

knowledge, **51**

Kotler, Phillip, 63

L

Lauterborn, Robert, 62, 63

LEFT( ) function, **9**, 10, 12, 23

letters, creating, 33–34

liabilities, **47**

liquidity, **44**

logos, adding to reports, 54

long-term liabilities, 47

lookup fields, 64

*Loyalty Effect and Loyalty Rules,
The* (Reicheld), 76

loyalty programs

creating, 76–77

described, **76**

M

Mail Merge, **27**

Mail Merge Wizard, using, 32

market research, conducting, 69–71

market segmentation, **59**

marketing
    developing target markets, 62–67
    flyers, creating, 76–77
marketing mix, **62**
mass marketing, **62**
matching
    data types, 5–6
    using SWOT analyses for, 69
math, common intrinsic functions (fig.), 10

N

named ranges, 25
naming queries, 10, 11, 53
Navigation Pane, 4
niche market, **62**
niche marketing, **62**
normalized (databases), **3**
Notes pane, 20
numbers, entering into validation rules, 52

O

online personas, 67
opening
    database tables, 4
    Expression Builder dialog box, 10
operational section of business plans, 79
opportunities (SWOT analysis), 70
order cost, **21**
organizations using target marketing, 60
Outlook, saving e-mail messages, 32

P

page numbers, inserting into reports,
        19–20, 35
parameter query, 30–31, 33
percent values, formatting, 16
performance criteria, 2
personas
    creating, 67–69
    described, **67**
photos, inserting, 77

PivotCharts
    automatic updating, 66
    forms, creating, 55
PivotTable Reports, 65–66
place (of four P's), 62
planning steps, **2**
planning steps to solve business problems, 2
Porter, Michael, 72, 74, 75
postcards, creating Mail Merge, 60–61
Power of the Persona, The (Rind), 67
PowerPoint
    creating business plan with, 80–83
    creating presentations with, 20–21
    starting, 27, 68
presentations, 35
    creating, based on report, 27, 35
    creating business plan, 80–83
    developing, basing on report, 20–21
price (of four P's), 62
primary keys, 7, 10
Principles of Marketing (Kotler and Armstrong), 63
problems. *See* business problems
product (of four P's), 62
pro-forma balance sheet
    creating, 47–48
    described, **44**
promotion (of four P's), 62

Q

queries
    adding field to, 8
    creating, 7–16, 23–24, 28–31, 53–54
    creating reports from, 53–54
    described, 51
    input boxes when running, 30
    saving, 15, 54
Query Wizard, 31

R

ranges, named, 25
record identifiers, 7
referential integrity, 5

Reicheld, Frederick, 76
relational databases vs. Excel, 51
relationships, **3**
    creating, 4–7, 23, 52
    updating, 57
Relationships window, 4–5
reorder point, **22**
reports
    completing inventory analysis, 26
    completing sales analysis, 19–20
    creating, 65
    creating from query, 53–54, 57–58
    creating presentations based on, 35
    information requirements, 8
    organization of, 19
    PivotTable, 65–66
reserved words (Access), 56
return on investment (ROI), **79**
rewards programs, 76
Rind, Bonnie, 67
ROUND( ) function, **10**

S
sales
    creating queries of month's, 8–10
    creating query of cumulative, 13–14
saving
    database tables, 52
    e-mail messages, 32
    forms, 55, 58
    queries, 10, 11, 15, 54
    reports, 65
    student files, 4
    Word documents, 32
slicers, inserting, 65–66
specialty coffee industry, Five Forces analysis for, 75
SQR( ) function, **10**
SQRT( ) function, **10**
Starbucks, 70
startup costs, **44**
strategic analyses, 72
strengths (SWOT analysis), 70
subforms, adding, 58

SWOT analyses
    described, **69**
    developing, 69–71

T
tables (database)
    building, 51–52
    creating, 56–58
    creating relationships, 4–7
Table of Contents
    inserting into presentations, 83
    inserting into reports, 19, 26
target market, **59**
    developing, 62–63
    identifying, 63
threats (SWOT analysis), 70

U
United States v. Microsoft, 74
updating
    databases, 64–66
    PivotCharts, 66

V
validation rules, entering numbers into, 52
Vehicle Identification Number (VIN), 10

W
weaknesses (SWOT analysis), 70
what-if analysis, **45**
Word
    completing report using, 26–27
    Mail Merge Wizard, using, 32
    marketing flyers, creating, 76–77
Word Advanced Options dialog box, 33
workbooks, performing analysis and charting, 17–19
worksheets
    adding to workbooks, 65–66
    inserting rows into, 18